Goldfish

Marshall Ostrow

Everything about Aquariums, Varieties, Care,
Nutrition, Diseases, and Breeding

With 32 Color Photographs and 64 Drawings

Consulting Editor: Dr. Matthew M. Vriends

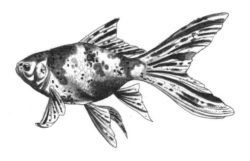

Woodbury, New York/London/Toronto/Sydney

All inquiries should be addressed to
Barron's Educational Series, Inc.
113 Crossways Park Drive
Woodbury, New York 11797

Paper Edition
International Standard Book No. 0–8120–2975–5
Library of Congress Catalog Card No. 85–4714

Library of Congress Cataloging in Publication Data
Ostrow, Marshall.
 Goldfish: everything about aquariums, varieties, care, nutrition, diseases, and breeding.

 Includes index.
 Summary: A practical guide for keeping goldfish, with information on aquarium maintenance, varieties of goldfish, their purchase and daily care, breeding, diseases, and outdoor pools.
 1. Goldfish [1. Goldfish] I. Title.
SF458.G6084 1985   639.3′752   85–4714
ISBN 0–8120–2975–5 (pbk.)

Front cover: Fantail
Inside front cover: Well aquascaped community tank with several varieties of goldfish.
Inside back cover: Well aquascaped community aquarium with several goldfish varieties.
Notice the filter tubes.
Back cover: (above left) Common; (above right) Fantail; (below left) Black moor; (below right) Shubunkin.

All photographs by William J. Presnal of Sayreville, New Jersey
All drawings by Steven Sabella of Commack, New York

PRINTED IN THE UNITED STATES OF AMERICA

567   ARC   98765432

Contents

PREFACE

Goldfish are one of the most popular pets in the world. Undoubtedly their brilliant metallic gold and reddish coloration is greatly responsible for that popularity. Their mild temperament, extreme hardiness, and lack of fussiness about food and water conditions also add to their appeal.

A clean, well-cared-for, and attractively decorated aquarium containing a few brightly colored goldfish swimming easily through plant thickets and around rock clusters is a fascinating and relaxing sight. However, in spite of their undemanding nature, it does take a little bit of work and some common sense to keep goldfish healthy, happy, and active. The purpose of this book is to help the novice goldfish keeper enjoy this relaxing hobby—without becoming involved in a lot of aquarium-keeping drudgery. While there is a certain amount of pleasure in the actual care of goldfish, I have always found the greatest joy in sitting back and simply watching my goldfish as they glide smoothly through the water, occasionally stopping to nibble on some tasty morsel or interact with one another in a flashy, yet easy, display of courtship or rivalry.

Enjoying goldfish in this way is not a twentieth century discovery, for goldfish were one of the first aquatic animals in recorded history to be kept as pets. They are mentioned in Chinese literature as far back as the seventh century A.D., when they were supposedly first domesticated and kept in various kinds of bowls and small pools. It is difficult to know exactly why goldfish were such desirable pets in ancient China, but it is reasonable to assume that it was their bright golden color and easy manageability, as it seems to be today, that made them so popular.

While goldfish appear to have originated in China, it was the Japanese who began to develop them several hundred years ago into the exotic forms and colors we see them in now. Through selective breeding, plain, common goldfish were transformed into strains having bright red, white, and satiny black colors, long flowing fins, exotic eye and body shapes, and some rather bizarre yet attractive growths around the head. So complete is the transformation of some of these strains, that the beginner may not be able to recognize them as related in any way other than color to the common goldfish from which they were derived.

This book explains how to choose an aquarium, select good quality goldfish, maintain a healthy aquatic environment, prevent, diagnose, and treat goldfish diseases, breed your goldfish, and keep them in outdoor ponds. A special section teaches you how to understand normal goldfish behavior. This book also discusses the physical and behavioral traits of most of the common goldfish varieties.

This book is dedicated to my mother, my wife, and my youngest son, Scott, who listened patiently as I put my ideas together. I believe that if you follow the suggestions offered in these pages it will take you no time at all to understand your goldfish and the simple care they require. Then you will have time to sit back, as I do, and simply enjoy them.

Marshall Ostrow

SELECTING A HOME FOR YOUR GOLDFISH

Unlike dogs, cats, and many other pets, goldfish cannot really share your home. Because they live in water and not on land, they must have their own self-contained environment. This is provided by keeping them in a fishbowl or an aquarium filled with water. Since you cannot just bring goldfish home and turn them loose in your house, you must first buy a container in which to keep them and set up the container. Once that is done, you may purchase the fish and bring them home.

Fishbowl or Aquarium?

There are two basic kinds of containers in which to keep goldfish—a fishbowl or an aquarium. A fishbowl is a round or bowl-shaped container; it usually has a capacity of one gallon (4 liters)* or less. An aquarium is a flat-sided container—a square, rectangle, hexagon, or other shape—and it usually has a much larger capacity than a fishbowl.

Advantages and Disadvantages of a Fishbowl

While a fishbowl does have a few advantages over the aquarium, they are mostly to the fishkeeper, not the fish. The fishbowl can be placed safely on almost any small surface. When full it can be moved easily from one place to another,

---

* Comparable metric measurements are given in parentheses throughout the book.

and, if not excessively aquascaped, it is easy to clean.

The most difficult problem with a fishbowl is that it can comfortably house only one or two small goldfish. Most experienced fishkeepers find that 1 gallon (4 liters) of water is about right for one small goldfish, and fishbowls are rarely available in sizes larger than a 1- or 2-gallon (4- or 8-liter) capacity. The nature of the problem, though, is not so much the size of the bowl or the amount of water it holds as it is the available water surface area. The goldfish breathes by using its gills to extract oxygen from the water and to expel carbon dioxide. Most of the oxygen in the water is absorbed from the atmosphere at the surface of the water, which is also where carbon dioxide wastes are released. Within limits, the more water surface area there is in the container, the more oxygen can be absorbed and carbon dioxide released.

Not realizing the importance of water

In a fishbowl that is filled up almost to the top, there is less surface area for the exchange of oxygen and carbon dioxide and the fish tends to go near the surface, gasping for air. In a fishbowl only half filled up, there is greater water surface area, more available oxygen, and the fish does better.

surface area, most inexperienced fishkeepers tend to fill their fishbowls almost to the top, probably assuming more water is better for the fish. They also fill up the bowl because it looks better full than half full. Because of the curvature of the sides of the fishbowl, however, the higher it is filled beyond the halfway point, the smaller the water surface area. Restricting the surface area reduces the exchange of oxygen and carbon dioxide, and thus the number and size of the fish that can be kept comfortably in the bowl.

Fishbowls can be nicely decorated with colored gravel, rocks, ceramic or plastic figures, and live or plastic plants. A decorated fishbowl, however, becomes a problem at cleaning time. Because of the small size of a fishbowl, the water tends to become more polluted than it does in a larger aquarium, and in less time. Cleaning a fishbowl therefore often requires the removal of all the water and every-

A small fishbowl can be made more comfortable for a goldfish by adding a filter, some gravel, and a few plants.

thing else in the bowl. The new water must then be conditioned to remove chlorine and other impurities; the gravel must be washed before putting it back in the bowl; and the plants and rocks must be cleaned and then rearranged in the bowl. Depending on how you care for your fish, all of this might have to be done as often as once a week, and it should be done, even with expert care, at least once every four to eight weeks. A larger aquarium, on the other hand, doesn't have to be thoroughly cleaned by dismantling it nearly as often. As a matter of fact, I am going to tell you further on in this book how to set up and maintain an aquarium so that it does not have to be taken apart for a thorough cleaning more often than once every five to ten years. A fishbowl is, of course, quite easy to clean if it is not aquascaped, but fishkeepers usually decorate their fish containers.

Most readers will probably decide on an aquarium rather than a fishbowl. Nevertheless, they should remember what we have just said, for even to an experienced aquarist a fishbowl is useful as a temporary fish container when cleaning the aquarium or as an isolation container when treating a diseased fish.

Choosing a Location for Your Aquarium

Throughout the rest of this book I shall be speaking of aquariums rather than fishbowls. Remember, however, that most of the information applies to the fishbowl as well as the aquarium.

Selecting a Home for Your Goldfish

Before buying your aquarium, give some thought to where you will place it, for this could dictate the size and shape of the tank you buy. Furthermore, once the goldfish aquarium is set up, it should not be moved. Moving a full aquarium could cause the glass to crack or a seam to leak, not to mention the harm that could come to the goldfish from being knocked into objects in the tank. In choosing a location for your aquarium you should consider the weight of its contents, access to an electrical outlet, the availability of sunlight, the temperature and draftiness of the room, accessibility for feeding and maintenance of the goldfish, ease of viewing, the amount of foot traffic passing by the tank, and accessibility and safety to small children and curious or hungry cats.

Weight
A 10-gallon (40-liter) aquarium containing a few rocks, an appropriate amount of gravel, and filled with water weighs about 100 pounds (45 kilograms). Should you decide to put the aquarium on a shelf or table, make sure they are sturdy enough to hold that much weight without warping or collapsing. If the shelf or table warps, stresses will be put on the aquarium. Eventually this could cause the side or bottom of the aquarium to crack suddenly or a seam to leak. Wrought iron or wooden aquarium stands, usually available where you buy the aquarium, are designed to hold the weight of the aquarium for which they are built.

Be sure the site you choose for your aquarium is level. Otherwise, as in the case of the warped shelf or table, the resulting uneven pressure will put stresses on the tank which, after a time, could cause it to burst open suddenly.

If you decide to buy a very large aquarium, such as the 55-gallon (220-liter) size, which, when full, weighs about 600 pounds (270 kilograms), it should not be placed in the middle of a room or even along an unsupported wall. The weight concentrated in a small area could cause floors to warp or sag. That, too, could eventually damage your aquarium.

Access to Electricity
You are probably going to have an aquarium light, a filter, and other electrical equipment to help maintain a healthy environment for your goldfish. Therefore, locate your tank close to an electrical outlet. Then you can probably hide the electrical cords behind the aquarium, out of sight. This will improve the appearance of the aquarium and its immediate surroundings and make the area safer, with no electrical cords exposed where they can be tripped over or destroyed by young children, dogs, or cats.

Light
Light is needed for your fishes' overall well being and as a source of energy for your aquarium plants. Now is the time to decide whether you want to illuminate your goldfish tank with natural sunlight, artificial light, or a combination of both. To take advantage of natural sunlight,

with or without the added benefits of artificial light, the aquarium must obviously be located near a window. The question of which window should be settled before the aquarium is set up. A south-facing window admits the most intense and longest number of hours of direct sunlight. Conversely, the weakest and least number of hours of direct sunlight comes from a north-facing window. An east-facing window admits moderately strong light, and a west-facing window admits moderately weak light.

The most sunlight is not necessarily the best arrangement, because excess illumination, be it natural sunlight or artificial light, can cause problems. For example, an excess growth of algae can result, coating all the glass as well as every object in the tank, including live plants. Algae-covered plants will die and pollute the aquarium water. Excess algae can also give the water a soupy green appearance. Another problem caused by excessive sunlight or artificial incandescent light, especially in an aquarium as small as a 5- or 10-gallon (20- or 40-liter) size, is uncontrollable water temperature. If the water temperature rises much above 75°F (24°C), your goldfish may not be very comfortable. This is partly because warmer water holds less oxygen than cooler water, and if the tank is crowded, the goldfish may not be able to get enough oxygen. Furthermore, at night a small tank may cool down too quickly. This could trigger a whole host of health problems.

For the best overall light conditions,

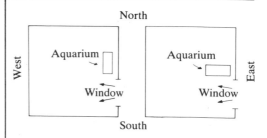

For the best light conditions, an aquarium should be placed near an east-facing window. Placing it parallel to the wall reduces the amount of direct sunlight it receives, thus helping to prevent erratic temperatures and excessive algae growth. Placing it perpendicular to the wall is even better, allowing the aquarium to receive lots of indirect sunlight.

the aquarium should be situated near an east-facing window. During the most intense days of summer sun, shades can be drawn to help keep the aquarium cool. During the winter more artificial light can be used to supplement the shorter number of hours of daylight. The aquarium should not, however, be located directly in front of the window. Rather, it should be off to the side, either parallel or perpendicular to the wall. This will help prevent overheating from too much direct sunlight during the summer and erratic temperatures from drafts during the winter.

Room Temperature and Ventilation
Make sure the room you choose for your aquarium is not drafty and is not subject to extreme changes in temperature from day to day or hour to hour. Avoid

locations near doors that lead directly to the outside. Trouble can also be avoided if the aquarium is not set up anywhere near a heat or air conditioning duct or near an air conditioner. Remember, unstable temperatures can cause unstable health in your goldfish.

Room for Servicing

Select a site for your aquarium that allows enough space above and behind to service it. How frustrating it can be to discover a month after you've set up your aquarium that because of an overhanging shelf you don't have enough working space to net out an ailing fish. You'll also need enough space above the tank to be able to reach your hand into it to use a siphon for removing debris or to remove a filter for cleaning. Later on you may want to change the decorative background behind your aquarium or simply clean the outside of the back glass. Neither one of these chores is easy to do if you can't put your arm behind your aquarium. You should have at least 8 to 10 inches (20 to 25 centimeters) of free space above your aquarium and about 5 to 6 inches (12 to 15 centimeters) behind it.

Position for Viewing

The aquarium should be placed at a height comfortable for viewing from either a standing or sitting position. A table or shelf height of about 30 inches (75 centimeters) is ideal—this is the height of most commercially made aquarium stands.

Foot Traffic and Safety

An excessive amount of foot traffic and swinging doors near your aquarium can spell disaster for your goldfish. A heavy traffic area increases the likelihood that someone or something will collide with the aquarium. If such a collision doesn't break the aquarium, it will at least startle the fish. Their reaction will be to dash around the tank, and they could injure themselves by colliding with the glass or with some object in the aquarium, such as a rock. Avoid setting up the aquarium in hallways or places where young children play. If the aquarium is to be set up for the benefit of young children, consider their activities and locate the aquarium accordingly.

The Right Aquarium

After you have decided where to place your aquarium, you can choose one that is right for you. It must be the right size and shape to fit the location you have chosen and the right size and shape for the number of fish you want to keep.

Almost all aquariums on the market today are all glass and frameless, except perhaps for a decorative plastic rim around the top and bottom which protects the glass from chipping. Such tanks are not too expensive, are easy to repair, and do not scratch easily.

Selecting a Home for Your Goldfish

Glass aquariums were once made with stainless steel, aluminum, or plastic frames, but these have largely disappeared from the market and you will not find them in pet shops. If you should be given such an old-fashioned framed glass tank, seek advice on how to clean it thoroughly and seal all the joints with silicone.

Plastic aquariums are generally available only in very small sizes. They break and scratch easily and the plastic walls often distort the image of the fish. They are not recommended. You can, however, consider purchasing a small plastic tank—they are cheap—to use as a quarantine tank when you need to isolate a diseased or injured fish for a short period of time.

What Size?

The size of your aquarium depends on where it will be located and on the number of goldfish you wish to keep. Your goldfish are going to need as much room as you can possibly give them. The more water you have per fish, the more dilute the accumulated fish wastes will be. This will help prevent diseases and promote proper growth. Also, the larger the tank, the less likely the goldfish are to suffer from an oxygen shortage.

A general rule of thumb commonly used to determine how many fish to put in an aquarium is: 1 inch of fish per gallon (about 6 or 7 millimeters of fish per liter) of water. Use this rule for young fish no more than 2 inches (50 millimeters) long

and be sure to include the length of the fins. Once the goldfish begin to grow, the rule no longer really applies, because goldfish are heavy-bodied creatures that consume more oxygen per unit of length than fish having a more streamlined shape. The slimmer species are probably the ones the rule was created for. In other words, keeping ten 1-inch (2.5-centimeter) goldfish in a 10-gallon (40-liter) aquarium will not allow much room for growth. This does not mean the goldfish will not grow; it merely means they will not reach their full potential size, and their fins and bodies may not develop into the most beautiful or desirable proportions. Stunting could also mean the goldfish may not be able to breed well.

Five young goldfish, each 2 inches (5 centimeters) long, would initially be ideal for a 10-gallon (40-liter) aquarium. After a while, though, when the goldfish grow to 3 or 4 inches (7.5 or 10 centimeters), they will be a bit crowded. So if you want to keep five goldfish, you would probably be better off starting out with a 15- or 20-gallon (60- or 80-liter) aquarium. You see, therefore, that the size of the tank you buy depends on the number of goldfish you wish to keep.

What Shape?

Aquariums of the same water capacity come in different shapes, and these different shapes vary in water surface area and thus in fish capacity. For example, suppose you are interested in buying a 20-gallon (80-liter) aquarium. This size

Selecting a Home for Your Goldfish

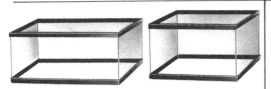

A 20-gallon long aquarium (left) has about 25% more water surface area than a 20-gallon high aquarium. With its greater gas exchanging capacity, it can hold a few more fish than a 20-gallon high tank or it can make the same number of fish more comfortable.

is commonly available in at least two shapes. Both are 12 inches (30 centimeters) wide, but one, called a 20-gallon high, is 24 inches (60 centimeters) long and 16 inches (40 centimeters) high, while the other, called a 20-gallon long, is 30 inches (75 centimeters) long but only 12 inches (30 centimeters) high. The water surface area of the long tank is about 20 percent greater than the water surface area of the high tank. Because of the greater surface area of the long tank, oxygen absorption and carbon dioxide release take place more quickly and in greater quantity, within the limits of the amount of water in the tank. Therefore, if you plan to fill a 20-gallon (80-liter) aquarium to its limit with fish, buy the long tank—it will comfortably house more goldfish.

While more will be said later in this book about the consequences of crowding goldfish, it is important to understand now, before you buy your aquarium, that crowding your fish may not only stunt their growth but may also cause serious health problems because of overpollution of the water. Crowding can also cause increased aggressiveness in your fish. This can result in injuries that could lead to bacterial or fungal infections and other serious diseases. Therefore, it is not advisable to stock any tank to its maximum capacity. In all my aquariums I've always kept fewer than half the recommended number of fish for each tank. This is probably the main reason why I've not had many diseased fish over the years. This may also be why I've had aquariums set up as long as ten years without having to dismantle them for a complete cleaning.

In summary, there are many practical reasons to select a location for your goldfish aquarium before you buy it. All these reasons point to one fact: moving an aquarium with water in it can cause the glass to crack or a seam to leak. When choosing an aquarium, buy the largest one you can afford. In a larger aquarium the goldfish wastes will be more diluted and there will be more oxygen available. This will increase the chances of your goldfish remaining in good health and growing to their full potential size.

AQUARIUM EQUIPMENT AND ACCESSORIES

Aquarium Cover and Light

You can keep your goldfish aquarium uncovered, but your goldfish will be a lot safer with a tight-fitting cover on the tank. While goldfish are not prone to jumping out of the water, as some fishes are, they are capable of some minor aerial acrobatics. They may leap out when startled or when the water becomes polluted. They may also leap out in an attempt to free themselves of gill parasites or other disease organisms. If the aquarium is covered, they will fall back into the water. If it is not, they may be injured by the fall to the floor and dried up by the time you find them. And, an added benefit: an aquarium cover not only keeps the goldfish in but also keeps other things out—unwanted things, such as airborne grease (from cooking) and dirt particles, cat's claws, and objects accidentally dropped into the tank.

When the aquarium is covered, less water is lost by evaporation. Water vapor from the aquarium water cools in the air over the surface of the water, condenses on the inside of the aquarium cover, and then drips back into the water. This helps

Most plastic light hoods have a hinged front to make feeding and caring for the fish easy.

cool the water, and that is especially important during the summer. It also helps keep the fish wastes in the water more dilute, making the environment healthier for the goldfish.

Most aquarium covers consist of a hinged front section that swings up for servicing the aquarium and feeding the fish. The rear section usually has an aquarium light built into it. The whole unit is called a *light hood*. A better quality hood has a glass panel built into the back section to prevent water vapor from condensing in the light fixture. This helps prevent electrical shorts and prolongs the life of the light fixture and the bulbs.

There are two basic types of light fixtures: incandescent and fluorescent. An incandescent fixture or light hood is less expensive to buy than a fluorescent hood, but it costs more to operate. It also produces a lot more heat than a fluorescent hood, which makes temperature control difficult, especially in a small aquarium. A fluorescent light hood is much cooler and much safer to handle.

Heater and Thermometer

Goldfish are coldwater fish. They thrive best at temperatures of 65° to 72°F (18° to 22°C). Some of the sturdier goldfish varieties, such as common goldfish, comets, moors, or shubunkins, can tolerate water temperatures close to the freezing point (32°F or 0°C), as long as the temperature does not drop by more than a few degrees a day. Even the less sturdy strains, such as lionheads, celestials, orandas, and others, can tolerate water temperatures in the low 60s (about 15°C), as long as the temperature is brought down slowly.

Because of the coldwater adaptability of goldfish, it is not absolutely necessary to put an aquarium heater in your goldfish tank. However, if you live in a climate in which the winters are very cold, your goldfish could be in trouble if your home heating system ever broke down. This is especially true if you have a small tank. Five or ten gallons (20 or 40 liters) of water can drop from 70°F (21°C) to 40° or 50°F (4° or 10°C) in just a few hours. A drop like this could throw your goldfish into temperature shock, making them very susceptible to certain diseases. Temperature shock can even kill them directly and rather quickly. I suggest, therefore, that you keep an aquarium heater in your goldfish tank, set at 65°F (18°C). This will protect your goldfish if the temperature drops below 65°F (18°C), but above that the heater will not turn on. If you don't keep a heater in your aquarium, you should at least keep one handy, so it can be used in an emergency.

A simple formula tells you what size heater you need for your aquarium. In general, you need 2½ to 5 watts per gallon (0.6 to 1.2 watts per liter) of water. For example, if you have a 10-gallon (40-liter) aquarium, use a 25-watt or a 50-watt heater. Aquarium heaters with built-in temperature controls are available in 25-watt to 200-watt sizes.

An automatic aquarium heater senses the water temperature and turns the heater on or off as needed. However, the unit does not indicate what the actual water temperature is. To know the temperature you must measure it with an aquarium thermometer. You should use a thermometer even if you don't have a heater in your aquarium. It will tell you if the water temperature is bouncing up and down too much or if it is too warm or too cold for your goldfish.

Aquarium thermometers are of two types: those that go inside the aquarium and those that stick on the outside of the aquarium glass. Inside thermometers either float free in the water, rest on the bottom of the tank, or hang down into the water. They are mounted in a plastic or stainless-steel bracket that clips over the edge of the tank. Inside types are not as safe as stick-on types, because they are made of glass and can be broken when bumped by a large goldfish. Stick-on thermometers, as the name implies, simply stick on the outside of the aquarium glass and accurately sense the water temperature through the glass.

Make sure the thermometer is not too close to the aquarium heater or in direct sunlight. Otherwise, it will give you erratic temperature readings.

Filters

Filtration is one of the most important and least understood aspects of aquarium keeping. Very few fishkeepers are successful without using some sort of filtering device in their aquariums. Deciding which filter to use, however, is not easy without understanding at least the basics of how filters work.

There are three kinds of filtration processes. Mechanical filtration is the process of separating suspended dirt from the water. It is accomplished by passing the water through a filtering medium such as a filter-floss pad. As the water passes through, the dirt is trapped in the pad.

The second process is called chemical filtration. Fish wastes pollute water and can change some of the chemical characteristics of it. Passing the polluted water through a bed of activated charcoal or carbon removes some of the dissolved pollutants from the water and helps restore the water to its original condition.

The third process is called biological, or living, filtration. It is the most difficult to understand but probably the most important. It is a process whereby two kinds of beneficial bacteria convert poisonous chemicals produced by fish wastes into other chemicals that are harmless to goldfish and beneficial to aquarium plants.

Types of Filters

Most aquarium filters provide at least two of the three filtration processes, and some provide all three. There are several common types of filters: box filters, power filters, and undergravel filters.

The Box Filter

A simple box filter provides complete filtration—mechanical, chemical, and biological. It consists of a small plastic

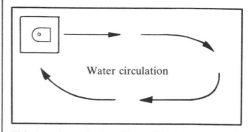

This top view of a box filter with the output tube extended to the surface and capped with a 90° elbow shows how complete water circulation is promoted.

box in which a riser tube or water output tube rises from a filter plate up through the lid. A layer of filter-floss and a layer of carbon are placed on top of the filter plate inside the box. An air hose from an airpump is connected to the water output tube, and the whole unit is placed in the aquarium. Air bubbles rising through the water output tube cause dirty water to be drawn into the filter box, where it passes

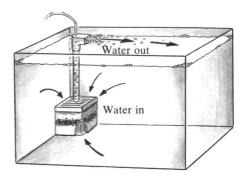

With the riser tube of a box filter extended to the surface cleaned water is carried away from the filter, thus promoting better water circulation and more efficient filtration.

Aquarium Equipment and Accessories

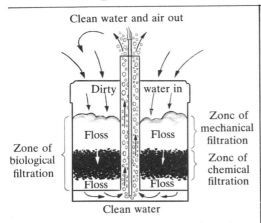

Clean water and air out

Dirty water in

Zone of mechanical filtration

Zone of chemical filtration

Zone of biological filtration

Floss

Floss

Floss

Floss

Clean water

This cutaway view of a box filter shows how the filtering materials are layered and where each filtration process takes place.

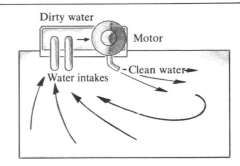

Dirty water

Motor

Water intakes

Clean water

This top view of a power filter shows the correct positioning of all the parts for maximum filtration and water circulation.

The Power Filter

Like the box filter, the power filter also provides complete filtration. In principle it works the same way as a box filter, but it is more efficient. Instead of being inside the aquarium, the power filter hangs over the edge of the aquarium, outside the tank. Water is moved through the filter by a powerful water pump rather than a

through the filter-floss and carbon layers, leaving dirt and some unwanted chemicals called ions behind. The cleaned water is drawn from under the filter plate, up the water output tube, and back into the aquarium. Mechanical separation of the dirt from the water takes place in the filter-floss, and removal of harmful ions occurs in the carbon layer. Billions of beneficial bacteria, which inhabit all surfaces of every fiber in the filter-floss and every particle in the carbon layer, carry out biological filtration. The bacteria, through a two-stage process, convert ammonia, which arises from goldfish wastes and is deadly to the fish, into nitrates, which are harmless to goldfish and very beneficial to aquarium plants. A box filter may clean 25 to 50 gallons (100 to 200 liters) of water per hour, depending on the size of the box filter and the size of the airpump.

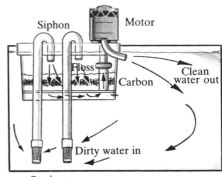

Siphon

Motor

Floss

Carbon

Clean water out

Dirty water in

Strainers

Maximum filtration and water circulation is achieved with a power filter by directing the clean water output across the surface and away from the intake tubes.

Above: common goldfish
Below: comet
These two varieties are hardy and good choices for a beginner.

▷

rising stream of air bubbles, as in the box filter. The power filter draws water out of the aquarium, through the filter-floss and carbon layers in the filter box, and back into the aquarium, trapping the dirt and harmful ions in the filter box outside the tank. A small power filter cleans water at a rate of about 100 to 150 gallons (400 to 600 liters) per hour. In a 10-gallon (40-liter) aquarium a power filter can recirculate all of the water 10 to 15 times in an hour, which is quite adequate. Power filters are available with flow ratings as high as 1200 gallons (4800 liters) per hour, which would be suitable for a 100- to 150-gallon (400- to 600-liter) aquarium.

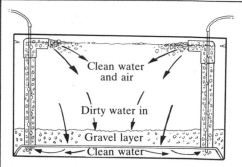

Complete circulation and maximum filtration is achieved in an undergravel filter by bringing the riser tubes to the surface and capping them with 90° elbows. For maximum output and best oxygenation the water level should be near the center of the elbow.

The Undergravel Filter

An undergravel filter provides the best biological or living filtration, and it also provides good mechanical filtration. Mechanically, it works the same way as a box filter. Dirty water is drawn downward through a bed of filtering material which lies over filter plates. In this case, however, the filter plates cover the entire aquarium bottom, and the filtering material is the aquarium gravel. A much larger culture of beneficial bacteria can develop in an undergravel filter than in a box filter, because all of the surfaces of each particle of gravel become home to huge colonies of bacteria. This means that poisonous ammonia can be disposed of much faster in an undergravel filter than it can in either a box filter or a power filter. As in the box filter, water is moved through the filter by means of air bubbles rising through water output tubes and carrying cleaned water with them.

Which Filter for You?

Although the box filter and the undergravel filter are much less expensive than a power filter, they require an airpump to run them. A power filter does not. In the end the cost is about the same.

The box filter does not recirculate water nearly as well as an undergravel filter or a power filter. It is best suited for use in a small aquarium, such as a 5-gallon (20-liter) size, or a large fishbowl. In a larger tank, such as a 10-gallon (40-liter) size, more circulation is needed to ensure that there is enough oxygen in the water and that all of the wastes reach the filter. If box filters are used in such a tank, two are needed.

In an aquarium of 10 gallons (40 liters) or more, an undergravel filter or a power filter of the right capacity should be used.

The undergravel filter should be used only if the aquarium is to be sparsely populated with goldfish, for it is not as good a mechanical filter as a power filter, and an accumulation of fish wastes on the bottom of the tank will eventually clog the undergravel filter and cause the entire system to become foul.

Many fishkeepers use an undergravel filter and a power filter, both at the same time. This provides the best possible mechanical filtration and the best possible biological filtration. It permits more goldfish to be kept in the aquarium. It also allows a very long time to pass (perhaps years) before the aquarium and its undergravel filter needs to be dismantled for a thorough cleaning.

Airpumps and Aeration Accessories

An airpump and other accessories that regulate the air supply to the goldfish are also necessary in an aquarium.

Airpumps
Many different kinds of airpumps are available from a small, inexpensive vibrator pump that is adequate for the operation of one box filter to a large compressor capable of operating an entire bank of aquariums. Choosing the right size pump is important, because one that puts out too much air causes filters to operate as inefficiently as one that does not put out enough air. The airpump should be capable of putting out a heavy stream of fine air bubbles for every water output tube and airstone it is to operate.

You should buy an airpump with about twice the capacity you presently see the need for. After you are successful with your first few goldfish, you'll probably want to add a few more fish to the aquarium. Having a larger pump allows you to add more filters or airstones, as the need arises. If the airpump is too powerful initially, the excess air can be bled off through a bleed valve. As your need for more air increases, the bleed valve can be closed.

If you have chosen an aquarium that is deeper than about 12 inches (30 centimeters), you'll also need more air to overcome the backpressure caused by the added water depth. Again, I repeat, buy an airpump that is at least twice as large as you presently think you need.

Airstones
An airstone diffuses the air from the airpump into many small bubbles in the aquarium. Many small bubbles have a much greater surface area than a few large bubbles. The greater surface area allows for increased absorption of oxygen from the air—and thus more oxygen for the fish.

Airstones vary in their size, shape, weight, color, and the fineness of the bubbles they produce. They are used to operate filters or alone, just to aerate the water, which makes breathing easier for the goldfish. The only characteristic of an airstone that is of any practical importance is the size of the bubbles it produces. Some airstones produce a fine mist of bubbles. This looks nice in an

19

Aquarium Equipment and Accessories

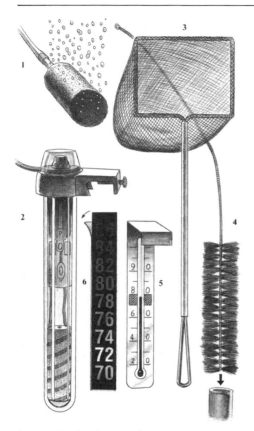

aquarium, but it does not produce enough turbulence at the water surface to adequately aerate the aquarium or lift enough water through the water output tube of a filter. A stone producing coarse bubbles about 1/16 of an inch (1.5 millimeters) in diameter gives the best overall results for filtration and aeration. It also helps your airpump last longer; the fine mist airstones cause back pressure that shortens the life of an airpump.

Air Valves

Air valves are needed to regulate the air supply to the goldfish and to the filter and to bleed off excess air from the airpump until it is needed in the aquarium. They are available as single valves or as banks of two to five or six mounted on a bracket than hangs over the edge of the aquarium. For a beginning goldfish keeper with his or her first aquarium, a bank of three valves is recommended; one or two valves to operate filters or a filter and an airstone, and one valve to serve as a bleed for excess air.

Air Hoses

Air hoses vary only in length. How much to buy depends on where the pump is to be kept in relation to the aquarium and how many air outlets the pump is to run. You'll need a single length of hose to run from the airpump to the bank of air valves, and then an adequate length for each airstone or filter to be operated. It seems that no matter how much air hose

Accessories for the aquarium
  1. An airstone, which diffuses the air from the airpump and helps aerate the water.
  2. An automatic aquarium heater that will prevent the water from dropping below a comfortable temperature for your goldfish.
  3. A fish net for moving the goldfish.
  4. Special brushes are available for cleaning debris out of the filter tubes.
  5. A stainless steel or plastic base thermometer that hangs in the water over the side of the aquarium.
  6. A modern digital thermometer that sticks on the outside of the aquarium glass.

Aquarium Equipment and Accessories

If the airpump cannot be kept above the water level of the aquarium, then the airhose should have several loops in it and the loops should be above the water level. This prevents water from back siphoning into the pump in the event of a power failure.

you buy, it is never enough. It is not very expensive, so to be safe, if your calculations indicate that you need 10 feet (3 meters) of hose, buy 20 feet (6 meters). Buy more than you think you need.

Gravel

Finally, you will need gravel for your goldfish aquarium. Gravel is available in a variety of colors, compositions, and particle sizes. Regular aquarium gravels are almost always color-fast, so there is no need to worry about the color fading and tinting the water or poisoning the goldfish. For goldfish, stay with a stone gravel—not sand, dolomite, or crushed coral.

Particle size is very important. If the gravel is very fine, it may pack down tightly as it begins to fill with debris. This chokes off air and water circulation through the gravel, and soon causes the gravel to become foul-smelling and polluted. It will then release gases into the water that could poison your goldfish. Tightly packed gravel also kills plant roots.

If the gravel particles are too large, pieces of uneaten food will fall between them. This organic debris will decompose and foul the aquarium. Furthermore, gravel that is too coarse will not provide adequate anchorage for your plant roots. This is no problem for floating plants, but rooted plants will die without proper anchorage.

A number three gravel, having a particle size of about ⅛th-inch (3-millimeter) diameter, is perfect for a goldfish aquarium. If you are using an undergravel aquarium filter, you will need enough number three gravel to provide a bottom layer about 2 to 3 inches (5 to 7.5 centimeters) deep. In a 10-gallon (40-liter) aquarium, for example, this will be about 20 to 30 pounds (9 to 14 kilograms). If you are not going to use an undergravel filter, you will need just enough gravel to give your aquarium plants sufficient anchorage or cover the bases of plastic plants. This will require about a 1-inch (2- or 3-centimeter)-deep layer of gravel—about 1 pound of gravel per gallon (1 kilogram of gravel per 10 liters) of aquarium capacity.

Fishnets

No aquarium keeper should be without a fishnet. The larger the net, the easier it will be to catch the goldfish without injuring them. All fish have a tendency to jump when lifted out of the water. A larger net will help prevent this, for there will be enough loose netting material to enable you to gently grip the goldfish with the material as you lift it out of the water. If you have, for example, a 10-gallon (40-liter) aquarium, a 6- or 7-inch (15- or 17-centimeter)-wide net will do the job.

Fishnets should always be rinsed and sterilized before putting them into the aquarium. This precaution will help prevent disease in your goldfish. Rinsing the net in hot tap water does not really kill the bacteria or parasites that may be in it. The net should be dipped into boiling water for about 20 seconds before each use. There are very few microorganisms that can survive 20 seconds of boiling water.

AQUARIUM PLANTS

Why Plants?

Your viewing pleasure and the comfort of your goldfish are important things to think about when setting up your aquarium. Both needs can be met by the generous use of aquatic plants.

The basic needs of goldfish are oxygen, food, and shelter. Aquatic plants can provide all three. Although, with the selected diet you'll be giving your goldfish, and with a good filtration and aeration system, food and oxygen are insignificant contributions of aquarium plants. The shelter provided by the plants, however, is quite important. To see this yourself visit a pet shop or the home of a friend in which there are well-planted and barren aquariums set up. In the bare tank the fishes' colors are washed out, their movements are more or less jerky, and they are easily frightened by the slightest bump to the aquarium. In the well-planted aquarium the goldfishes' colors are much more brilliant, their movements are smooth and easy, and they are not easily frightened. In other words, a thickly planted background apparently makes the goldfish feel more secure. If they are more secure, they are under less stress. Under lower stress their natural disease resistance is much higher.

As far as your own enjoyment is concerned, you'll find a well-planted aquarium much more pleasant to look at than a barren one. The planted aquarium has a more natural appearance, and it may even enhance the appearance of the room it is situated in. Furthermore, healthier, happier goldfish look a lot better. The green background provided by the plants brings out sparkling brilliance in the metallic oranges and reds of the goldfish. The goldfish are likely to get along better with one another, eat better, and generally be more active overall. In addition, a planted background, more so than a bare tank, is likely to help trigger spawning in mature goldfish. Having fish reproduce is indeed one of the more pleasurable aspects of aquarium keeping, even if you don't raise the fry (baby fish).

Plastic Replicas or Live Plants?

Many fishkeepers find that growing plants in a newly established aquarium is rather difficult. I agree that if you don't have the right kind of plants it isn't easy. This is because the water and the gravel in a new aquarium—new being defined here as any aquarium set up for less than six months—has not had time to build up a supply of nutrient materials. Plants not having a large self-contained storehouse of nutrients will die of starvation in a few weeks in a newly set up aquarium. However, there are some plants that can do well in a new aquarium. You will have to decide whether to try growing them or to use plastic plant replicas.

Plastic Plant Replicas
The easiest, although expensive, way to solve the problem of dying plants in a newly set up aquarium is to use plastic plant replicas. There are several manufacturers of plastic plant replicas whose

Aquarium Plants

products so closely resemble the real thing that without close scrutiny most people looking into an aquarium can't tell the difference. To the goldfish, of course, it makes no difference at all, since, as pointed out earlier, you provide them with choice foods and your filtration and aeration system provides them with all the oxygen they need. All the goldfish really need from plants in an aquarium is a fairly dense, dark background, and that is indeed provided by plastic plant replicas.

Aside from the fact that no special conditions of light, temperature, and water chemistry are required to maintain plastic plants, they have another important advantage over live plants—they cannot be destroyed by your goldfish. Goldfish are omnivorous creatures—that is, they eat both animal and vegetable matter. It is not uncommon to see goldfish nibbling away on the tender young leaves of aquarium plants. While you may see goldfish nibbling on the leaves of plastic plants, they are usually nibbling at the algae that grow on them or on the microorganisms that live among the algae fibers. Goldfish soon learn that they cannot eat the plants themselves, and eventually they stop trying. Meanwhile, during this "learning" period, your plants will not be destroyed.

Live Plants for the New Tank

The best plants to use in a newly set up aquarium are those species that have heavy rhizomes, or rootstocks. The rhizome is the part of the plant from which

the roots and leaf stalks grow and is the part in which most of the plant's food supply is stored in the form of starch. Plants such as *Aponogeton*, some *Echinodorus*, and some *Cryptocoryne* species have thick rhizomes. Because these plants contain vast food stores in the rhizomes, they can be put into a newly established aquarium and will survive if kept under the right conditions. On the other hand, plants that lack heavy rhizomes, common and decorative species such as *Vallisneria*, most of the *Sagittaria*, *Hygrophila*, and *Myriophyllum* (parrot's feather), will not do well in an aquarium that has not had a chance to build up a concentration of minerals in the water and in the gravel bed and are best avoided until the aquarium has been established for about six months.

To grow aquatic plants successfully you must pay attention to their environmental needs—just as you pay attention to the needs of your goldfish. You must consider the temperature, water conditions, and lighting required for the plants.

Needs of Plants

Most of the aquatic plants available to the aquarium hobby are tropical species. Some are flexible in their temperature requirements, but many are not. If your goldfish aquarium is being maintained at room temperature—about 70°F (21°C)—the plants you choose should be those species that do best at temperatures of 65° to 70°F (18° to 21°C).

Water chemistry is also important.

Aquarium Plants

Some plants only grow well in acidic water—that is, water having a low pH value such as 6.2, for example. Since goldfish do not do well in such water, these kinds of acid-loving plants, including most of the *Cryptocoryne* species, should be avoided. Most of the plants that grow well in very alkaline water—water having a pH value over 8—also thrive well in water that is very slightly acidic (pH value of 6.8), neutral (pH value of 7.0), or water that is mildly alkaline (pH value of 7.2 to 7.6). The latter is the condition of most city water supplies and is the pH value at which both goldfish and most aquatic plants thrive. The extremes are mentioned here only because water in an aquarium tends to become more acidic over time, especially if a careful maintenance program is not followed. (More will be said on this in the chapter "Aquarium Maintenance").

Light conditions are also critical to the survival of aquarium plants. Without light of sufficient intensity and duration, aquarium plants will die. Natural sunlight is one of the best sources of light for aquatic plants. As we said before, however, most aquarium plants are tropical species. This means they require about 12 hours of light a day. This is more than the sun provides during the winter in a temperate climate like that of the United States. Natural sunlight must therefore be supplemented, especially during the winter, by artificial light. This, of course, is done with a lighted aquarium hood.

The kind of bulb used in an aquarium hood is very important. There are fluorescent tubes that give off a pinkish, purplish glow that enhances the colors of your fish and plants, making them and even the rocks look brilliant. However, these kinds of fluorescent lights are only intense enough to promote plant growth in a small, shallow aquarium, such as the standard 5- or 10-gallon (20- or 40-liter) size. Most larger aquariums are too deep for the light to penetrate the water sufficiently. In a larger aquarium you can use a Warm White® or a Vita-Lite® bulb. These cover a broader part of the spectrum and are much more intense. Their light penetrates deeper water, and they promote good plant growth. Cool White® bulbs are also bright enough, but they give everything an eerie, washed out appearance.

Incandescent lights promote excellent plant growth, but to use them you must have an incandescent fixture. With these fixtures there is a tendency to use bulbs that are larger than necessary. Remember, the higher the wattage, the more heat they produce, and this could cause a water temperature problem in a small tank.

Do aquarium plants need fertilizer? If, as suggested, you use only plants with their own built-in food supply when you first set up your aquarium, there is no need to fertilize the gravel bed. By the time these plants have consumed their own food supply there will be, thanks to bacterial action in the gravel bed, more than enough nutrients in both the gravel and the water to keep these plants flourishing. It is best, therefore, that the beginner use an unfertilized gravel bed as a plant-growing substrate.

Aquarium Plants

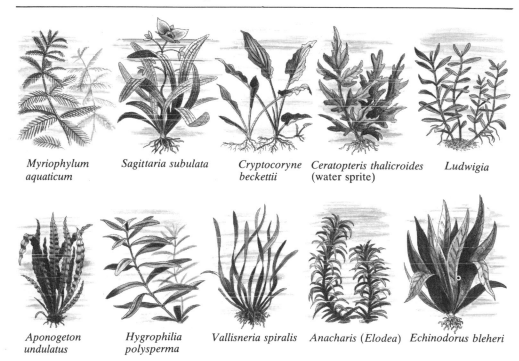

Myriophylum aquaticum

Sagittaria subulata

Cryptocoryne beckettii

Ceratopteris thalicroides (water sprite)

Ludwigia

Aponogeton undulatus

Hygrophilia polysperma

Vallisneria spiralis

Anacharis (Elodea)

Echinodorus bleheri

Arranging Aquarium Plants

Tall bushy varieties are best used as background plants in the rear corners of the tank and along the back. They can be arranged in front of heaters, filter tubes, air hoses, and box filters, so that they hide these unsightly items. Other varieties of shorter plants can be placed in front of the background plants to provide, as it were, a natural progression of height toward the back of the aquarium. This progression creates a well-balanced overall pleasing effect, and it leaves the goldfish plenty of open swimming room at the front of the tank where they will be more visible most of the time. If, at times, the goldfish need more seclusion, they can swim through the plant thickets or hide behind them.

Plant Varieties for the Aquarium

There are quite a few commonly available plants (and a few uncommon ones) that do well in a new, nutrient-poor, relatively cool (unheated) aquarium.

Aquarium Plants

Java Fern

One of the easiest plants to grow in an aquarium is the Java Fern (*Microsorium pteropus*). This plant has a thick rhizome that produces light-green to dark-green leaves shaped like elongated spearheads. The rhizome grows along the surface of whatever the plant becomes rooted to—which can be the gravel, a piece of driftwood, or even a rock—and new leaves arise from the rhizome. The leaves can be as long as 8 or 9 inches (20 or 23 centimeters), but in the cool water of a goldfish aquarium they will only grow to about 4 inches (10 centimeters). This plant, therefore, makes a nice foreground decoration. It comes from India, southern China, and the Indo-Malayan area as far as the Philippine Islands, where it is an amphibious species, growing right up out of the water along the trunks of partially submerged fallen trees. A unique feature of Java Fern is that it can thrive in dim light or bright light, and it can tolerate acidic or alkaline water, as long as extremes are avoided. It does well in a normal range of aquarium temperatures, from a low of about 68°F (20°C) to a high of about 80°F (27°C).

The rhizome of Java Fern should be weighted down on the gravel surface with a small rock, but it should never be imbedded in the gravel. It can also be tied to a piece of driftwood or a rock, with a piece of monofilament fishing line. Eventually the roots will attach to these surfaces. It reproduces by extending the rhizome horizontally, with the leaf stalks growing straight up out of it. If a piece of a broken leaf is anchored down, it will produce a new rootstock or rhizome, and new leaves will sprout from it. Unfortunately, this beautiful plant is not seen in the hobby as often as its ease of cultivation would indicate. However, it is worth seeking out for use in a newly established aquarium.

Water Sprite

The water sprite (*Ceratopteris thalicroides*) is a commonly available aquatic fern that is also extremely versatile in its requirements. It grows best in acidic, shaded water, but it also grows quite well in normal aquarium water in a moderate, but not excessive, amount of light. It has deeply forked bright green leaves. Like Java Fern, it reproduces by developing buds right on the leaves. The leaves are quite fragile, but almost any small fragment is capable of producing new leaf buds. Because water sprite is so soft and fragile, goldfish may eat large amounts of it. This is not a problem, though, because the plant usually grows faster than most fish can consume it. Water sprite grows in a floating form, which reproduces so fast that it quickly covers the water surface with a dense layer of small plants. The weak, bushy roots can be imbedded in the gravel. In its planted form the leaves become more deeply divided or forked. Temperature requirements range from a minimum of 68°F (20°C) to a high of about 80°F (27°C).

Cryptocoryne

Several species of *Cryptocoryne*, which are sometimes known simply as crypts, are commonly available. All crypts come from tropical Asia, and they are generally not tolerant of temperatures below 70°F (21°C). Some crypts are amphibious, while others are completely aquatic. Marsh species, such as *C. becketii* and *C. nevillii*, are often grown in domestic aquatic nurseries. They are small foreground plants with narrow spear-shaped leaves that rarely exceed 6 inches (15 centimeters) in length. Of these two, the easiest for beginners to handle is *C. becketii*. It grows in almost any water and can tolerate strong or weak light. It can tolerate a water temperature as low as 70°F (21°C) without much adverse effect on its growth. It reproduces easily by sending runners out of its thick rhizome, or rootstock. It is a good plant for a new aquarium.

Aponogeton

Aponogetons are good plants for the new aquarium because they have a thick tuber that contains a vast food supply which can sustain the plants for months in a nutrient-poor aquarium. However, once the food supply is used up and the tuber begins to rot, the plant is not very easy to bring back to good health. If good aquarium maintenance is practiced, there is usually sufficient nutrient material in the tank before any serious tuber rot occurs. The common aponogetons, such as *A. undulatus* and *A. natans*, have leaves that are long and undulate (curled or crinkled) along their edges. The plant thrives well in almost any normal aquarium water and can tolerate temper-atures as low as 60°F (16°C). At that cool a temperature, however, the leaves fall off and the plant goes into a dormant state. New leaves begin to grow when the water temperature rises into the high 60s (approximately 20°C).

Swordplants

Swordplants (*Echinodorus* species) are found almost exclusively in South America, especially in Brazil. One of the easiest to grow in almost any aquarium, new or old, is *E. osiris*. It has large, bright-green leaves that are elongate and spear-shaped, like those of the crypts, but they are proportionately much broader. The leaf blades have strong veins and can grow to a length of 12 inches (30 centimeters). The plant grows well in a new aquarium because it has an unusually heavy rhizome for a swordplant. It is tolerant of temperatures as low as 65°F (18°C). This plant requires very strong overhead light. A single *E. osiris* makes a spectacular central focal point in an aquarium. The Amazon swordplant (*E. blehri*) looks very much like *E. osiris*, except that it does not have much of a rootstock. Although quite popular in fish stores, it should not be planted in a new aquarium. Another species, *E. cordifolius* (formerly known as *E. radicans*), is well suited for a new tank. It grows large, oval, light-green leaves on long, thick stems. Sometimes the leaves grow out of the water, but this can be prevented by using less light. This species also makes a magnificent centerpiece plant.

Aquarium Plants

Rooted plants such as this *Vallisneria* species should be planted with the white crown above the gravel.

Vallisneria and Sagittaria

These are two very popular groups of aquarium plants, the latter also being known as arrowheads. Both have long, narrow, ribbonlike leaves with very short stems or no stems at all. They all require strong light. They are so popular because they make excellent background plants, easily concealing aquarium equipment such as heaters and filter tubes. They reproduce by sending out runners from the bottom of the crown, which is the white part at the bottom of the leaves. Like all of the rooted plants discussed so far, they should be planted with the white crown showing just above the gravel surface.

Corkscrew val (*Vallisneria spiralis*)—val is a common name for *Vallisneria*—is probably the most popular in this group of rooted plants. Its narrow, ribbonlike leaves grow upward in spirals—hence the name corkscrew. It grows wild in the southern part of the United States and is therefore well suited to the temperatures in a goldfish aquarium. It grows quite well in normal aquarium water. However, because it has a very small rootstock, it should not be used until the aquarium has aged for a few months.

Various *Sagittaria* species, known by the common name sag, grow in most of the tropical and temperate zones of the world. Two have become quite popular in the aquarium trade, the most common being the dwarf sag (*S. subulata*). The narrow bladelike leaves grow to a length of 2 to 3 inches (5 to 7.5 centimeters). In strong light the plant quickly spreads by means of runners, forming a nice green carpet, so to speak, in the foreground of the aquarium. The plant is extremely versatile in its water requirements and grows well in a nutrient-poor aquarium, because it has more of a rootstock than most other *Vallisneria* or *Sagittaria* species. *Sagittaria graminea* is the other sag species commonly used in the aquarium. Its leaves are proportionately broader than those of the dwarf sag and reach a length of about 10 to 12 inches (25 to 31 centimeters). It too, grows well in a medium that is not very rich in nutrients and in water of almost any composition.

Banana Plant

The underwater banana plant is quite popular in the aquarium hobby. It is an American plant that grows in shallow water. The "bananas" are actually tubers that form the rhizome. The plant is merely dropped to the bottom of the aquarium, where, after awhile, it grows adventitious roots that anchor it in place. In weak light the plant grows round leaves, about 2 to 3 inches (5 to 7.5 centimeters) across, on short stems. In strong light, however, the stem grows to the surface, where it sprouts a round wide leaf that floats on the top of the water and looks like a miniature lily pad. Because the plant contains so much stored food in the "bananas," it thrives quite well in a new aquarium.

Nonrooted Bunched Plants

This group includes several large families of plants that take nearly all of their nourishment directly from the water, through their leaves. They grow mostly adventitious roots. They are sold as cuttings that are bunched together and are usually planted in the aquarium that way. Some hobbyists prefer to let them just float free in the aquarium. Because they require a nutrient-rich environment, they usually fall apart quickly in a new aquarium and leave quite a mess.

Once the aquarium is sufficiently aged (about six months), anacharis, also known as elodea, or ditch moss, adapts quite well to the cool temperatures of a goldfish aquarium. Its highly branched stems can reach a length of over 3 feet (1 meter), even in a small aquarium, by growing around the tank in a tangle. The plants are useful as a background, because they can be trimmed to the height of the aquarium (which is true of most of the nonrooted plants). Anacharis is a dark green color.

Cabomba, popularly known as fanwort because the leaf whorls look like lacy fans spread around the stems, is a very delicate plant that easily falls apart, especially in the presence of goldfish which are likely to nibble at it. I do not suggest it for the goldfish aquarium.

Of all the bushy nonrooted plants, *Myriophyllum*, commonly known as water milfoil, is by far the hardiest. It can tolerate almost any aquarium conditions, as long as there is nutrient material in the water. Because of its extreme bushiness, long winding and branching stems, and its dark green color, it is an excellent background plant. Left in tangled clumps, it is a favorite spawning site of goldfish and is favored by goldfish breeders. The thick bushy structure prevents the adhesive eggs of goldfish from being shed freely into the water, where they can be more easily devoured by the fish.

Hygrophila polysperma is one of the most frequently seen cut, bunched plants. Its light-green leaves grow out of stem nodules in pairs, usually 180° apart. Alternating leaf pairs grow perpendicular to one another, so that looking down from the top of a stalk the leaves seem to come out in four directions 90° apart. The plant does not branch much, although branching can be promoted by pruning. The plant can tolerate most aquarium water and takes cool temperature quite well. When cuttings are planted in a moderately rich medium, they grow dense thickets of white roots. It is assumed, therefore, that this plant takes some of its nourishment from the substrate as well as some directly from the water. The plant is recommended as background if it is allowed to grow to the surface, and as foreground if it is trimmed short. Its only drawback is that it requires very strong light. In weak light it just falls apart.

Ludwigia, another cut, bunched plant frequently seen in aquarium stores, is very similar in all respects to *Hygrophila*, except that its leaves tend to take on a reddish color, especially on the underside. It should be handled the same way as *Hygrophila*.

The list in this chapter is far from complete, and once your goldfish aquarium is well established, there are many other varieties of plants that can be used. No matter what plants you choose for your aquarium, in the end it all comes down to understanding what you are doing and being patient. An aquarium full of flourishing plants cannot be established in a few weeks. It may take a year or more for the plant life in your aquarium to develop as you want it. The wait, however, is worth the reward, for if good maintenance practices are followed, it is not inconceivable that a well-planted aquarium can go on almost indefinitely without being broken down for a complete cleaning.

SETTING UP THE AQUARIUM

Preparing the Equipment

Begin by washing out the aquarium. *Never use hot water*, as it can cause the glass to crack. Room-temperature water or cold water is fine. *Never use soap, detergent, or any other cleaning compound* in your aquarium or on any of its equipment. A tiny bit of overlooked soap or detergent concealed in a corner of the aquarium or perhaps under the plastic rim and then dissolved in the aquarium water is more than enough to poison your goldfish.

A strong salt solution can be used to sterilize your aquarium. Six tablespoons of salt per gallon (or about 1½ tablespoons per liter) of water does the job. The aquarium and all the equipment—the filter, thermometer, heater, rocks, ceramic castles, and so forth—should be soaked for about an hour in the salt solution. Everything should be rinsed thoroughly before the aquarium is filled. Use paper towels, not laundered cloths, to dry your aquarium and equipment. A laundered cloth may have some residual soap in it that could end up in the aquarium water.

Putting the Tank in Place

Fasten the decorative background, if you are going to use one, to the back of the aquarium before you begin to set up the tank. Molded plastic three-dimensional aquatic scenes are available for each standard size aquarium. There are also available an assortment of colored foils. The foil background can be given a three-dimensional effect by wrinkling it into a ball and then stretching it out before taping it to the back of the aquarium. To allow for the wrinkles, buy a piece of foil that is longer than the aquarium, so that when it is straightened out the foil will cover the entire back glass.

Once the background is in place, the aquarium can be placed in the location you've chosen for it. Be sure to take all the precautions pointed out in the first chapter: keep the aquarium away from heat ducts and air conditioners, place it close to an electrical outlet, and far enough away from the wall for servicing.

Installing the Filter

If you are going to use an undergravel filter, it should be placed in the aquarium before the gravel is put in. The water output riser tubes should be adjusted to a length that brings the elbows at the top of the tubes halfway out of the water. This position provides the best water circulation and aeration. If you are going to use a box filter, you'll probably want to conceal it behind rocks or plants. It should therefore be put into the aquarium after the gravel is put in. If you are going to use a power filter, it should be the last piece of equipment installed after the tank is filled with water.

Setting Up the Aquarium

Aquascaping

Decorating your aquarium—aquascaping—will not only make the tank more attractive it will also make the goldfish more secure and happier.

Gravel

A lot of your aquarium's final appearance depends on the gravel—its color, size, and arrangement. Light-colored gravel or gravel close to the color of your goldfish will obscure the fish by giving them a washed-out appearance. Dark gravel, especially black or brown, will enhance and complement the colors of your goldfish. Dark blue or dark green gravel will also complement the fish. As I said earlier, the best gravel for a goldfish aquarium is number three gravel, having a particle size of about ⅛ inch (3 millimeters).

The gravel should be thoroughly washed (even though it comes from the dealer already washed) before it is put into the aquarium. This can be done in a clean bucket—one that has never been used for soap or detergent. A new bucket is safest, and it should be kept for aquarium use only. Run water through the gravel, stirring it constantly, until all the fine, dustlike particles mixed with the gravel are washed away. This should be done, of course, in a laundry tub or outdoors. Gravel can also be washed by scooping a small amount at a time into a fishnet or a kitchen sieve and running tap water through it until the water runs off clear.

Gravel sloped downward toward the front center of the aquarium makes maintenance much easier.

Gravel can be placed in an aquarium in a way that makes maintenance much easier. Make the gravel layer deeper at the back and sides of the aquarium than at the front. In other words, the gravel should be sloped downward toward the front center part of the aquarium. With this arrangement, pieces of uneaten food, fish droppings, decayed and broken plant leaves, and other kinds of debris tend to accumulate in one place at the front of the tank, where it can easily be siphoned off. With this method small plants need not be confined to the front of the aquarium, but can be planted "high up" on the slope.

Rocks and Other Decorations

Decorative rocks must be of a relatively hard, nonporous material; otherwise they could pollute the water and poison your goldfish. Red shale, slate, and hard sandstone are generally safe rocks to use in an aquarium. Soluble rocks such as lime-

Above: fantail with reddish orange coloring (left) ▷
and calico fantail (right).
Below: a community tank with several fantails.

stone should be avoided as they gradually dissolve and change the chemical nature of the water to a composition that is not healthy for goldfish. Petrified wood is also safe. Safe rocks and treated pieces of driftwood can usually be purchased at pet shops.

Never use seashells or pieces of coral as decor in a goldfish aquarium. Dissolved particles from these materials tend to make the water very alkaline, a condition that is not healthy for goldfish. In addition, particles of uneaten food tend to become trapped in the pores and crevices of shells and corals. This material will decompose and foul the aquarium water. Shells and corals also have lots of sharp edges that could injure goldfish when they brush by them.

Driftwood can be used as decoration in a goldish aquarium. However, the process of cleaning and curing driftwood to make it safe for aquarium use is complicated and time-consuming. If the store from which you buy your aquarium and goldfish does not handle cured driftwood, it is best to drop the idea of using it.

Ceramic items, such as castles, treasure chests, and shipwrecks, improperly cured can also poison your aquarium water. The same applies to plastic items glued together with the wrong kind of cement. It is best to buy these items only in stores that sell aquariums and related equipment.

There are a few other precautions you should take in using rocks to decorate your aquarium. Avoid rocks with extremely sharp edges: they could injure startled goldfish. Avoid piling rocks in such a way that a slight bump of the aquarium starts a miniature landslide. Not all goldfish are capable of getting out of the way fast enough, and they could be hurt. Avoid large piles of rocks if an undergravel filter is being used, for the rocks will block circulation through the gravel bed, and the filter will not work very well.

Rocks look best when they are grouped or clustered rather than scattered all over the aquarium. Some variety should be used in each group, but the differences should be limited mainly to size. Shape and color can vary somewhat but on a gradual scale. For example, in a group of three or four rocks the size can vary from 2 or 3 to 6 or 8 inches (5 or 7 to 15 or 17 centimeters) across, and all can be more or less round- or smooth-edged. A mixture of rounded and jagged rocks, however, does not look very good together. The same idea applies to color variety. In a group of three or four rocks, several shades of brown rock will look fine together, but a yellow, a brown, and a red rock just don't seem to belong together.

The location of rock groupings and driftwood is important to the overall appearance of the aquarium. A high stack of rocks or a tall piece of driftwood does not belong in the middle of the aquarium where it will have a tendency to carry the viewer's eyes up and out of the tank. Placed toward the rear and the side of the aquarium, however, a pile of rocks carries the eyes right toward the center of the tank. Small rocks usually look best at the front of the tank and should gradually

34

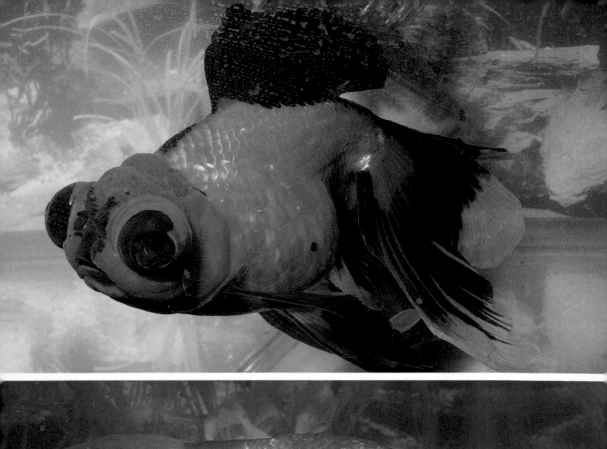

◁ Many varieties of goldfish have unusual eye formations.
Above: telescope with large eyes mounted on stalks.
Below: celestial, with eyes staring upward.

increase in size toward the rear of the tank. Plan your rock, plant, and driftwood arrangements with focal points in mind, but not too many focal points—one or two will do nicely.

Filling the Aquarium

After the rocks and other decorations have been placed on the gravel and air hoses connected to filters and airstones, the aquarium can be partially filled with water—coolish or room-temperature tap water. In terms of acidity (pH), hardness, and other characteristics, the tap water in almost all areas is suitable for goldfish, which are very adaptable animals. If the fish are not to be added immediately, even dechlorination of the water is not necessary, for the chlorine will dissipate within 24 hours.

At this time it is best to fill the aquarium about ¾ full. By not filling the

Filling a decorated aquarium improperly will uproot plants and disturb the aquascape. Fill it by aiming the water at a rock to disperse it.

tank to the top you can put your hands into the water to plant live and plastic plants and perhaps rearrange some of the rockwork without spilling water over the edge of the tank. The water should be poured over one of the larger rocks in the tank rather than directly on the gravel. This prevents the gravel from being stirred up and the decorations from being knocked over. You can also prevent this chaos by pouring the water into a small bowl or plate temporarily placed on top of the gravel.

Now the plants can be added to the tank. For the same reasons that tall rocks should not be placed at the front of the aquarium, neither should tall plants. With live plants, however, there is also an additional reason. Light (room light and sunlight) usually comes from the front of the aquarium, and tall plants up front will prevent light from penetrating to the plants behind them. Plants should be grouped the same way rocks are grouped, with an assortment of sizes but not different kinds in the same cluster.

With everything in place, the aquarium can be filled the rest of the way. Fill it to the bottom of the top plastic rim. The water line will then just disappear under the rim. Final adjustments of the top parts of the riser tubes can be made at this time.

Installing the Remaining Equipment

The thermometer can now be put in place. If it is the stick-on type, be sure the glass is absolutely clean and dry at the point of contact. Otherwise, the thermometer will not stay on, and the temperature readings will be erratic. Be careful where you stick it on, for once it's on it is there to stay.

Air hoses should now be connected to the valves and from the valves to the airpump. Where the pump is placed could be important. If it is at all possible, the pump should be placed higher than the top of the aquarium—for example, on a high shelf. In the event of an electrical blackout, this will prevent water from back-siphoning up the air hoses and down into the pump, which could ruin the pump. If the pump has to be placed lower than the top of the tank, the air hose should be looped above the water level several times (like a coil spring) and then run down to the pump. The loops can be held in place on top of the aquarium with a wire bag tie.

Once the air system is started up, you may find that the airstone and the box filter have a tendency to rise to the surface. This can be prevented by burying a section of the air hose under the gravel or under a rock.

Your aquarium heater should be anchored to the plastic rim of the aquarium at a rear corner of the tank. After it is plugged in the pilot light will come on if the heater turns on. This means that the heater temperature is set higher than the temperature of the water. Since it is to be used only as a safeguard if the water temperature drops below 65°F (18°C), the heater should be turned off by lowering the set point. This is done by rotating the dial on top of the unit to the left, or counterclockwise. If the water temperature is already at 70°F (21°C), a quarter turn of the dial should bring the set point down to about 65°F (18°C).

Finally, the hood can be placed on the aquarium. Don't forget to clean and sterilize the inside surface of the hood, just as you did the aquarium and its contents. Paper towels soaked in the same kind of salt solution used earlier is the safest way to clean the hood. Another paper towel soaked with fresh water is used to clean off the salt residue. Most hoods have holes or spaces cut in them to accommodate the installation of air hoses and heaters. If not, they have plastic inserts that can be easily cut to accommodate accessories.

Starting Up the System

Most new fishkeepers are eager to put their fish in the tank just as soon as it is set up. More often than not, however, this brings nothing but trouble. The tank is not yet biologically established; that is, the ammonia-destroying bacteria have not yet taken hold. The water temperature is probably not yet right. The fresh tap water is full of chlorine, and that can be very harmful to your goldfish. Although the chlorine problem can be easily and immediately disposed of by the addition to the water of a few drops of liquid chlorine remover, this does not solve the other problems. No matter how careful you are, netting goldfish out of their aquariums in the store, bagging them, transporting them home, and putting them in your aquarium is a traumatic experience for them. That trauma will be even worse if the aquarium you put them is not really ready to receive them. This whole ordeal could throw the goldfish into shock, which minimizes their chances for survival. I strongly recommend that you wait at least a week—two weeks would be even better—before buying your goldfish and putting them in your aquarium.

Meanwhile, here is what to do to prepare the aquarium for its new residents:

1. Start the filter and make sure it is operating correctly. There should be a good strong flow of water coming from the filter, and the filter's outflow should be as close to the surface of the water as possible.

2. Plug in the heater, and adjust it to cycle on and off at about 65°F (18°C). This may take a bit of time, but it will allow you to determine if the thermometer is working properly. Follow the manufacturer's directions for adjusting the heater.

3. Turn the aquarium light on, but don't leave it on all the time. It should be turned off when you go to bed and turned on again in the morning.

4. After 24 hours of filter or airstone operation, the chlorine will be gone, and it will be safe to "seed" your aquarium with some of the beneficial bacteria mentioned earlier. A good source for the bacteria is the shop from which you bought all your equipment. Ask them to give you a handful of gravel from one of their established aquariums. Most will readily accommodate you. Mix that gravel with the gravel in your aquarium. If it's not the same color as yours, just scoop some of yours aside, and bury the handful of new gravel under yours. Now you can buy one inexpensive baby goldfish, and put it into your aquarium. It will produce enough ammonia to feed the bacteria you have added to your tank and help establish the colonies of beneficial bacteria in your aquarium. All of this will work and should be done, no matter what kind of filter system you have. Most new aquariums tend to get cloudy after the first few days. This is because unwanted bacteria types are trying to become established in the water. The introduction of the "right kind" of bacteria will overcome this problem in a few days. The cloudiness will gradually clear if you keep the filter operating. When it clears, your aquarium is "ripe," and ready to receive its new residents.

By all of this I am not saying you cannot add your goldfish to the aquarium as soon as it is set up. Nor am I saying that if you do, they will definitely die. What I am saying is that your goldfishes' chances for survival without becoming ill are very greatly increased by waiting a week or two for the aquarium to become established before putting the goldfish into it.

GOLDFISH VARIETIES

Few aquarium fish have been developed in as many varieties as the goldfish. It has been estimated that there are over 125 varieties, and most of them were developed by Oriental breeders from one species—the Crucian carp. The Crucian carp has a metallic, yellowish, brassy color, which is not nearly as brilliant as its aquarium-dwelling cousin, the goldfish. In form it most closely resembles the common goldfish, which is short-finned, has a long streamlined body, and is compressed from side to side. That is where its resemblance to the goldfish stops.

Today's goldfish are seen in an array of flashy yellows, reds, and golds, as well as stark white, blues, purples, and a velvety black. Some have a variegated or speckled pattern. Some have very long fins that hang down like gossamer drapes. Some have fins that are split or doubled. Others lack a dorsal fin. Some have egg-shaped bodies with high rounded backs. Some have brightly colored fleshy growths around the head, eyes, nostrils, and gill covers, while others have the growth only around the nostrils. Some goldfish have huge eyes set at the ends of stubby cone- or telescope-shaped tubes or stalks that protrude from the head. Some have eyes that bulge from the head and constantly stare upward. Others have bulgy eyes that are surrounded by large fluid-filled sacs. Some goldfish have various combinations of these traits.

Because there are so many goldfish varieties with so many different combinations of traits, it is not possible to describe them all in a short book of this type. Furthermore, it is not practical to discuss them all, for many are very delicate and rarely seen in the hobby. When they are available their prices are prohibitive for most novice goldfish keepers. Therefore I will describe those varieties that are most commonly available and relatively easy to care for. After you have had some experience you may want to seek out more exotic varieties or even develop some of your own. As a matter of interest I have given the Oriental names for those varieties known to have been developed in the Orient.

For ease of understanding I will describe these goldfish in two categories: those with elongate compressed bodies and those with rounded or egg-shaped bodies. Some of each type have long or fancy fins, and some of each type have short fins. Only the egg-shaped types have fleshy head growths or hoods and unusual eye formations.

Flat-Bodied Goldfish

Common Goldfish

Several of the elongate compressed varieties are excellent choices for a novice.

In ancient China these were known as *Chin-yii*. In Japan they are known as *Kingyo*. Common goldfish are the basic fish described in the chapter "Understanding Goldfish." A good specimen is a bright orange metallic color. It has a wide (top to bottom), short (front to back) head and smooth body lines that taper evenly from its back and belly to its caudal (tail)-fin base. The caudal-fin base, or caudal peduncle, is about the same width as its snout, measured just in front of its eyes. The fins are stiff enough to be held fully erect. The caudal fin is moderately forked. The dorsal, or back, fin begins at the highest part of the fish's back and extends along the back almost to the beginning of the narrow caudal peduncle. When held erect, the outer edge of the dorsal fin appears smooth and slightly concave.

This is a hardy goldfish that eats well and can swim fairly fast. It tolerates mildly polluted water better than most goldfish varieties. It has a high tolerance for very cold water and therefore can survive well in an outdoor pond. In an average 10-gallon (40-liter) aquarium, if well cared for and not crowded, the common goldfish can grow to about 4 inches (10 centimeters). In a large un-crowded tank, it can reach 7 or 8 inches (18 or 20 centimeters), and in a spacious pond it can grow to well over 12 inches (30 centimeters). The common goldfish is an excellent choice for a beginner.

Comet

This is another hardy strain that can be kept in an aquarium or an outdoor pond. In body shape it is nearly identical to the common goldfish. Its fins, however, are much longer, especially the caudal fin. In a good specimen the caudal fin is almost as long as the fish's body, but it can still be held erect. The caudal fin is deeply forked, and the lobes are sharply pointed. The fish is usually a deep reddish orange metallic color but sometimes can be more yellowish. The comet is occa-sionally found with nacreous (pearly) scales, giving it a variegated color. It is a fast swimmer and a good feeder.

The comet doesn't grow nearly as large as the common goldfish. In a spacious aquarium or a pond it grows to a length of about 7 inches (18 centimeters), although exceptional fish are known to reach 10 inches (25 centimeters). The caudal fin elongation begins in young fish about 2 inches (5 centimeters) long, making it easy to distinguish young comets from young common goldfish. The comet is also an excellent choice for a beginner.

Shubunkin

In China this goldfish is known as *Chu-wen-chin*. It was supposedly developed in Japan about 1900, where it was called the *Shubunkin*, the name that has stuck with it throughout the Western World. The shubunkin almost always has a speckled or variegated color pattern. It is often referred to as a calico goldfish. It has nacreous scales that reveal an array of colors such as yellow, orange, red, brown, black, blue, purple, gray, and white. The more blue color the shubunk-in has the more valuable it is.

There are two kinds of shubunkins, the London shubunkin and the Bristol shub-unkin. The London type is almost iden-tical to the common goldfish, except, of course, for the color. Also, it is a smaller fish, rarely growing to more than 6 inches (15 centimeters). The Bristol type is similar to the London in shape and size,

Goldfish Varieties

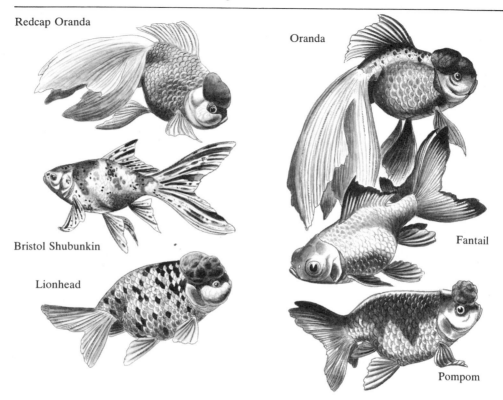

Redcap Oranda

Oranda

Bristol Shubunkin

Lionhead

Fantail

Pompom

except that it has an enormous tail fin that is very wide and not long like the caudal fin of a comet. The caudal fin is moderately forked and has wide well-rounded lobes. Of the two types, the London is seen more often. Both shubunkins are hardy strains that are strong swimmers and competitive feeders. They are recommended for beginners, especially the London type.

Egg-Shaped Goldfish

An egg-shaped goldfish has a short, stubby body with a very wide (top to bottom and side to side) head. In fact, it is difficult to tell where the head stops and the body begins. The entire fish—head and body—has the shape of an egg. The back slopes up from the head and is very high and rounded. Past the center the back slopes sharply downward toward the caudal peduncle. The caudal pedun-

Goldfish Varieties

Veiltail Ryukin

Water Bubble Eye

Celestial

Black Moor

Pearlscale

Calico Telescope

cle is short and narrow and is angled downward. Most of these goldfish have a split or double caudal fin, and good specimens also have a double anal fin. Because of its body shape, the egg-shaped goldfish has a distorted swim bladder, which sometimes causes it to swim at a head-down angle. These fish are not strong swimmers.

There are many varieties of egg-shaped goldfish, which can be grouped into two basic types: those with a dorsal fin and those lacking a dorsal fin. In those with a dorsal fin, the fin is usually very high and is often convex along the top edge, rather than concave as in flat-bodied goldfish. In those lacking a dorsal fin, a good specimen has a well-rounded, smooth back with no bumps or notches. A poor specimen may have an irregularly flattened back that is bumpy and sometimes notched; it may even have one or two small spikes sticking out of its back, which are vestigial dorsal fin bones that are only partially developed. The cumbersome body of the dorsalless goldfish has no "keel" to stabilize its motion, so its swimming ability is even poorer than that of the egg-shaped goldfish that has a dorsal fin.

With only a few exceptions, egg-shaped goldfish are not very competitive in aquariums of mixed varieties, unless all varieties are of the egg-shaped type. For the most part they are not hardy fish. They have a lower tolerance for pollution than that of flat-bodied types, and most cannot tolerate temperatures much below 60°F (16°C).

Fantail
The main distinguishing feature of this variety is its split or double caudal fin, which is of moderate length and slightly forked. In a good specimen the division is complete, but the two top lobes are much closer together than the bottom lobes. In other words, when looking at the fish from behind, its tail appears to circum-

The Ryukin has a high curved back that is almost discontinuous from the round egg-shaped body.

scribe an open triangle. In poor specimens the upper lobes are joined along the top edge or may not be split at all. The latter gives the tail a tri-lobed appearance, and the fish will not win any prizes in a competitive fish show. In a good specimen the anal fin is also double, with complete separation of each side. Even young good-quality fantails have complete separation of the anal and caudal fin divisions.

Fantails are available in metallic, nacreous, and matt scale types. In other words, they can be solid reddish orange, speckled, or whitish. The metallic-scaled type is the hardiest and most competitive fantail. It is one of the few egg-shaped goldfish that can be kept with flat-bodied varieties and hold its own where feeding is concerned.

There is a commonly available Japanese version of the fantail called the *Ryukin.* It has an extremely high curved back which seems almost discontinuous from the rounded egg-shaped body. Also, it has a wider caudal fin than a fantail. The tail is so wide that the top and bottom edges almost form a right angle with the body. Both fantails and ryukins grow to about 6 inches (15 centimeters), including the tail. Both are recommended for the beginner, especially the fantail.

Veiltail
This fish was derived from the Japanese *Wakin,* a double-tailed goldfish with an elongated body like a common goldfish. The veiltail looks a lot like a fantail,

Goldfish Varieties

A veiltail goldfish. Notice the double caudal fin. The anal fin extends back between the left and right lobes of the doubled caudal fin.

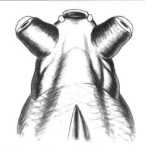

A dorsal view of the stalked eyes of a telescope goldfish.

except that it has extremely long delicate-looking fins. The dorsal fin, while long, is usually held erect, and it has an extremely convex outer edge. The double caudal and anal fins are well separated. Its body is a bit rounder than a fantail, and accordingly, its swim bladder is a bit more distorted. It usually grows to about 6 or 7 inches (15 or 18 centimeters), of which 3 to 4 inches (7.5 to 10 centimeters) comprise the tail. Like the fantail, it is available in all three scale types and hence a variety of colors.

It is ironic that the veiltail, thought of by most goldfish fanciers as one of the most beautiful strains, is also one of the weakest. Its delicate fins are very subject to injury and subsequent fungal and bacterial infections. Its extremely distorted swim bladder is very sensitive to chill. The veiltail should be kept only with other veiltails or other extremely noncompetitive varieties. It is not a good fish for a beginner.

Telescope

This is indeed an unusual fish. It has large eyes mounted on the ends of telescopelike or conelike stalks. In an adult specimen its eyes can be as far away from its head as ¾ of an inch (19 or 20 millimeters). It is believed that this fish was developed in China early in the eighteenth century where it was known as dragon eyes or the dragon fish. By the end of the century it was being produced in Japan, where it was and still is called *Demekin*.

Except for the eyes and its slightly smaller size, the telescope closely resembles the fantail. It is available in metallic- and nacreous-scaled types but rarely in matt-scaled. It usually reaches a length of only 4 inches (10 centimeters). It is not an extremely hardy fish, although it is not all that weak. Its biggest problem is that it doesn't see very well and thus it is not a good competitor for food. As a youngster this is not a problem, because its eyes don't begin to protrude until it is nearly six months old. It should be kept only with less competitive fish.

There is also a veiltail version of the

telescope. As if veiltails and telescopes don't have enough problems of their own, the combination of these traits results in a very weak fish, one that should be kept only by experienced fishkeepers. Even though it is not as weak, the short-finned telescope is not recommended for beginners either.

Moor
The moor is basically a black version of the telescope. It is known in England as the blackamoor. Its eyes usually don't protrude quite so far as those of the telescope. In a good specimen its color is a uniform velvety jet black. One of the surprising things about the moor, despite its telescopic eyes which are subject to injury and infection, is its hardiness. It has a high tolerance for low temperatures. In fact, it is recommended for a beginner if it is not kept with highly competitive fish. Indeed, it even does well in a small fishbowl, which can also be said of the fantail but of no other egg-shaped fish. The moor is also a good outdoor pool fish.

A dorsal view of the telescope eyes of the black moor. The eyestalks of the moor are rounder than the truncated eyestalks of the telescope.

The head growth of the oranda usually covers only the top of the head rather than the whole face, as it does in other strains.

Oranda
In Japan this fish is known as *Oranda Shishigashiri*. The oranda is very similar to the veiltail, the only significant difference being the oranda's head growth, or hood. This is a fleshy, pulpy-looking growth that develops mostly on the top of the head and somewhat on the sides of the head. This growth begins to develop when the fish is about 2 or 2½ years old. The growth is soft but not as soft as it looks, and it is not very easily torn. The hood is, however, subject to infection from debris, bacteria, and fungi that can settle in the tiny folds of the growth. With one very common exception, the oranda is seen mostly in the metallic-scaled type, with the color varying from a brassy yellow to a rich cherry red, all with the typical metallic gleam.

The variety with the color exception is easily recognized and difficult to pass by. It is called the redcap oranda. This fish is usually stark white, except for the hood which is a deep cherry red. Even young fish of this strain are easily recognized, for their colors are generally fixed at an early age. The amount of red on the head may change a bit, but usually there are no other color changes on its body. Later on, when the hood begins to develop, it grows only in the cherry red area. Unfortunately this gorgeous fish is as delicate as any veiltail and should be kept only by experienced fishkeepers.

Lionhead

Of all the dorsalless goldfish the lionhead, or *Ranchu*, as it is known in Japan, is by far the most popular and the most common. The lionhead is one of those cumbersome fish that lacks a stabilizing dorsal fin. It will not win any races to the mess hall. Nevertheless, a good specimen kept with other slow-moving varieties can get enough chow to thrive quite well. The fish is fully grown at about 5 inches (12 or 13 centimeters), and has short fins with a double caudal and anal fin.

The lionhead's broad head, except for its mouth, nostrils, and eyes, is completely covered by a fleshy head growth. Supposedly someone thought the fleshy hood looked like a lion's mane—hence the name lionhead. I personally think that the fish looks more like a huge raspberry with fins. However, since beauty is truly in the eyes of the beholder, don't let this author's bias thwart you if you find this or any other unusual goldfish attractive. Just remember that the lionhead is a very delicate fish and should be handled accordingly. It is not recommended for beginners.

A dorsal view of the head of a celestial goldfish. Notice how the eyes are fixed in an upward stare.

Celestial

One of the most unusual goldfish ever developed, the celestial is named for its bulging eyes that stare unalteringly upward. Thus it is known by the Chinese as the stargazer. It is believed to have been developed in China, as a goldfish with at least partially mobile eyes. The Japanese received it at about the turn of this century, and through selective breeding locked its eyes forever on the heavens. In Japan it is known as the *Deme-ranchu*.

In size, general form, and delicateness the celestial is very similar to the lionhead, having no dorsal fin. It does not, however, develop a hood. Most often seen in the metallic-scaled form, it occasionally pops up in the variegated nacreous form. It, too, is not a beginner's fish.

Water-Bubble Eye

Here is a goldfish that can only be described as bizarre. It is dorsalless, double-tailed, and quite similar in size and shape to the celestial. Its eyes are also turned upward but not as severely. What makes it so bizarre is that when the fish reaches about six to nine months of age, it begins to develop fluid-filled sacs under and around the eyes. By the time the fish is two years old the eye sacs are huge and look like two balloons being dragged around in the water by a fish. When the eye sacs are fully developed it is almost impossible for this bizarre creature to see anything, and it can barely even swim. The eye sacs break easily, heal slowly, if at all, and are highly subject to infection. For obvious reasons this all too commonly available goldfish is not recommended for community aquariums or for beginners.

And a Cousin—the Koi

In some fish shops you might see a whiskered cousin of the goldfish, the koi. Koi are known in the trade as Japanese colored carp. Of koi it has been said by some hobbyists that these are the only goldfish that are not goldfish, and it's true. Even though they look like goldfish, koi are not goldfish. Why are they mentioned here? Because some people mistake them for goldfish and erroneously mix them with goldfish in small aquariums.

Koi are derived from a different species of carp than the one from which the goldfish is derived. Most carp have whiskers, or barbels, and so do koi. Koi are bred on huge farms in Japan and have become in themselves a billion dollar industry. At Japanese auctions some breeder koi bring prices as high as $100,000.

The basic colors of koi are quite similar to those of goldfish but not the color patterns. Most koi are not one solid color. Their colors are variegated, but not often speckled as in the shubunkin. Rather, their red, orange, yellow, black, blue, and white colors form large patches seen mostly on the head, back, and upper flanks. The background color is often white, but not the stark white of the redcap oranda. Japanese breeders developed koi this way so their magnificent color patterns could be seen from above as the fish swim in ponds.

The feeding and breeding habits as well as the environmental requirements (i.e., temperature, water composition, etc.) of koi are nearly identical to those of goldish, but they grow much larger. Most fancy goldfish varieties rarely grow any longer than 5 or 6 inches (12 or 15 centimeters). Common goldfish grow to about 10 or 12 inches (25 or 30 centimeters), or occasionally to 15 or 16 inches (37 or 40 centimeters) if kept in a large uncrowded pond. Koi, on the other hand, normally grow to about 18 inches (45 centimeters), and if reared in a huge pond, it is not at all unusual to see koi over 3 feet (nearly 1 meter) long. Obviously koi require too much space to be kept in an ordinary aquarium. While it is hard to resist buying these beautiful fish, resist you must, especially if you are a beginner with a small aquarium. Any aquarium under 100 gallons (400 liters) capacity might be too crowded for a few koi by the time they are about one year old.

SELECTING GOLDFISH

Now you have your aquarium set up, have decided what type of plants to use, have learned a bit about the common goldfish breeds, and you're eager to get started. Where should you buy goldfish? How can you be sure to get good quality fish?

Find a Good Pet Store

One of the best ways to select good goldfish for your aquarium or pond is to find a store that is known for its quality and variety. Beware of bargain-priced fish—they are usually accompanied by bargain-priced diseases. Goldfish should be purchased either from private breeders who are experienced hobbyists or from reputable pet shops that are known for quality.

The first question that pops into my mind when I visit a pet shop is, "Is the store clean?" If the store is dirty, with merchandise strewn all over the place, you can almost bet the insides of the aquariums will be no cleaner. Look around the aquariums to see if there are any dead fish on the floor. If there are more than a few and you see uncovered aquariums the fish have probably been exposed to insecticides such as roach killers. If the fish aren't sick now, they probably will be soon.

Next, look into the aquariums. Are there any dead fish? There are bound to be a few in any store, because the personnel cannot be everywhere at the same time. If you see more than just a few dead fish, and especially if you see

more than one in any aquarium, be suspicious. The fish are probably not being well cared for. If the water in any aquarium has a tint of any kind, the fish in it are being medicated for some kind of disease. That's all right if it's only a few tanks. Even experts have fish that become ill. It's important, though, that the dealer readily admits that the fish are being treated for disease and is not willing to sell fish from those tanks. Not all medications tint the water, so you must be tricky. If you want fish from a particular tank, ask the dealer what the tank is being treated with, not whether or not it is being treated. Also, when looking over the tanks, beware of cloudy or foul-smelling water. Something is bound to be wrong with fish from such tanks.

Look for Signs of Disease or Injury

Now look for signs of diseased or injured fish. Are the fish in any tanks gulping air at the surface? Do they have clamped fins? Are any of them swimming erratically or lying on their sides at the top or bottom of the aquarium? Are any fish rubbing or scratching themselves against objects in the aquarium? Do any of them have torn fins? This may be unavoidable in some tropical species, so find out what kind of fish they are before making any judgments about torn fins. If they are peaceful fish, be suspicious that they are developing fin rot, a highly contagious disease that can spread to goldfish if they are handled with the same net.

Do any fish in the store, especially the

ones you want, have any noticeable diseases such as ich, velvet, fin rot, mouth or body fungus (white cottony tufts), clouded eyes, or bloody streaks in the fins and bodies? Are there any missing or roughed up scales, sores, or ulcers? Are there any unusual bumps or protuberances on the bodies and fins? Do any fish have consumptive (hollowed) bodies? If any of these signs or symptoms exist in any of the tanks, avoid buying fish from those tanks. If any of these things exist in more than two tanks, you had better buy your goldfish from some other store.

Ask the dealer lots of questions about care and maintenance, and question any irregularity you see in any tank. If the dealer refuses to answer your questions or answers them suspiciously, find another shop, no matter how good you think the fish may look. There is a reason for the dealer's evasiveness. It is not difficult to sell diseased fish to a beginning fishkeeper.

Avoid Stunted Fish

How do you avoid buying stunted goldfish? It's not always easy, but there are telltale signs. For example, in the flat-bodied varieties the profile of the body shape should be smooth. If you see a 2-inch (5-centimeter) fish that has a bumpy or bent body profile, you are probably looking at an old stunted fish. If you see full fin development on small comets, shubunkins, or veiltails you are probably looking at old fish. In hooded strains you should not see any hood development on any fish under about 2

inches (5 centimeters) and very little on fish between 2 and 3 inches (5 and 8 centimeters). If you see what appears to be premature hood development, it is probably not premature. These fish are likely to be old and stunted. Small telescopes or celestials should not have well developed eye features, as these features do not develop in very young fish.

Avoid Deformed Fish

Look at the fins of the fish you are selecting. Are they shaped normally for the strain? Are there any unusual indentations on the leading or outer edges of the fins? If there are, this is a sign that the fish may have been injured or diseased and has healed. Such malformations are most likely to be seen on long-finned varieties. The fins of these strains rarely grow back as they originally appeared. While such fish may now be perfectly healthy, they are certainly not as attractive as fish with normal finnage.

Some inbred strains carry gill cover malformations. The gill covers may be turned up on the outer edges or partially missing. This is sometimes accompanied by a deep indentation at the isthmus, which is the fleshy part of the throat where the bottoms of the gill covers meet. While such deformed fish may be perfectly healthy now, sooner or later they are likely to develop breathing difficulties, which could lead to all sorts of diseases.

Avoid fish with deformities of the mouth or spine. These defects tend to make the fish less competitive. They may not grow properly and could suffer from malnutrition.

One Variety or a Mixture?

An aquarium of mixed varieties is called a *community aquarium.* All the goldfish in a community aquarium should be compatible with one another. Each one should be able to compete successfully for its share of food and living space. Two main types of differences should be avoided: size discrepancies and combining slow and fast swimmers.

By and large, goldfish are peaceful creatures. Large goldfish do not normally bully medium-sized goldfish so long as both are competitive. Several very small goldfish, however, may have a hard time getting much food in the presence of three or four large specimens. Use common sense with regard to size discrepancies.

The more serious problem is pitting active strains against slow-moving strains. For example, lionheads or veiltails cannot move very fast compared to comets, shubunkins, or fantails. If these varieties are mixed in an aquarium, the lionheads, for example, do not get the lion's share of the food. In fact, they may not even get a kitten's share. Keep slow-moving strains only with other slow-moving strains.

Mixing Other Species with Goldfish

For the most part mixing other species—whether fish or other animals—is not recommended. Most other aquarium fish species are tropical and therefore require warmer water. Furthermore, many of them are territorial and aggressive. Angelfish, for example, which all too commonly show up in goldfish tanks, stake out a territory and viciously attack any intruders. Angels, they're not!

Another problem in mixing coldwater fish with tropicals is the communication of diseases. Most fish are carriers of diseases that do not affect them specifically but do affect other species. Goldfish could infect tropicals just as easily as tropicals could infect goldfish.

In theory other coldwater species could be mixed with goldfish, but cross infection would still be a problem. Furthermore, where do you get them? Pet shops rarely carry them, so you have to catch them in the wild. In most states this is illegal without a collecting permit. Collecting permits are usually issued only to scientists who can verify that their collections are related to their scientific investigation. Collecting without a permit, you may subject yourself to expensive fines and/or imprisonment. Most fish and wildlife departments are very strict in the enforcement of their regulations.

Some hobbyists have tried nonfish species with goldfish. Examples are turtles, frogs, crayfish, salamanders or newts, and freshwater clams. Cross infection could also be a problem here. Furthermore, most nonfish species are fish eaters, and will devour your goldfish at their earliest opportunity. Clams present two problems. It is difficult to tell when they are dead or merely inactive. By the time you determine they are dead, they have already begun to decompose and foul the water. In addition, their offspring are microscopic-size free-swimming organisms that parasitize the gills and bodies of fish. After a certain time they drop off the fish and become full-fledged clams. Larval clams are called glochidia and are dangerous to most fish.

The only other species that can safely be mixed with goldfish are koi—but only in a very large aquarium or pond. Other than koi, no other species should be kept with goldfish.

Selecting Pond Fish

Apply the same standards of quality you would apply to aquarium fish, and refer to the chapter on "Goldfish Varieties" to know which varieties are suitable. The main criterion is temperature tolerance. Shallow unshaded ponds can become quite warm when exposed to direct sunlight in the summer. Ponds also become quite cool when the weather cools. In spring and autumn small ponds are subject to extreme daily temperature excursions. The fish kept in ponds must be extremely hardy and tolerant of wide temperature fluctuations.

The best goldfish for ponds or pools are common goldfish, comets, and shubunkins. Koi can also be kept with these varieties. These fish can be kept in an outdoor pool all winter, as long as the pond is deep enough to prevent it from freezing to the bottom. In seasonal pools—that is, pools from which the fish

are removed in the winter—moors and fantails will also do quite well.

Left: orandas; a young oranda without a head growth ▷ (top); an oranda with some head growth (center); and an adult oranda showing a full hood (bottom). Right: pompoms; a young pompom without nasal growth: (top); 2 views of adult pompoms with fully developed nasal growths (center and bottom).

AQUARIUM MAINTENANCE AND DISEASE PREVENTION

The easiest way to keep goldfish healthy is by preventing their diseases rather than curing them. If asked why goldfish become ill, most people would probably agree that it is because they are attacked by disease-causing organisms such as bacteria, fungi, and viruses. While that is what happens, it is the result, not the cause. To find the real reason for goldfish becoming ill, let's rephrase the question to "When do disease-causing organisms successfully attack goldfish?" The answer is, disease organisms are most successful when goldfish are in a weak or stressed condition.

Many different kinds of disease organisms—for example, those that cause white-spot disease or fin rot—are always present in most aquariums, no matter how healthy the aquarium appears to be and no matter how well it is maintained. These organisms often lie dormant (inactive) until conditions become right for them to grow and multiply. A weak or stressed goldfish is the right condition. Environmental stress (foul water, crowding, poor diet, etc.) causes a goldfish to shed some of its protective body slime. The body slime is a mucus coating that normally protects fish from invading infectious disease organisms. When part of that coating is shed, parasitic and disease-causing organisms have a much better chance of successfully attacking the goldfish.

Environmental stress can be eliminated with a good aquarium management program. A good management program is complicated and does not require a lot of work. In fact, the object of a good aquarium management program is the elimination of most of the work of aquarium maintenance. Let's see what constitutes a good program.

Buy Good-Quality Equipment

Equipment failures are one of the causes of disease in aquarium fish. For example, if an automatic heater fails, one of two things can happen. Either the heater doesn't come on when a temperature drop calls for it, or it comes on and stays on, overheating the water. Even if your goldfish live through the ordeal, they will be weakened and susceptible to attack by any disease organism that happens to be in your aquarium.

One of the best ways to prevent or at least reduce the chances of equipment failure is to buy good-quality equipment. Begin with the aquarium itself. A cheap aquarium is usually made with thinner glass and less cement in the seams and is much more likely to crack or leak than a better-quality tank. A good-quality heater is more reliable than a cheap one, and it provides steadier temperature control. A cheap airpump does not produce enough air to operate filters at their maximum efficiency and is usually much noisier than a better-quality airpump. Blockages in the air system, such as a dirt-clogged airstone, usually cause a cheap airpump to break down a lot sooner than a better-quality airpump. Cheap filters might seem to turn over a lot of water, but most of them actually provide inadequate water circulation.

◄ Above: bubble-eye, a variety with fluid-filled sacrs around the eyes.
Below: lionhead, a variety with manelike head growth.

It is not necessary to buy the most expensive model of every item in order to maintain your aquarium properly. Be aware, however, that bargain-priced equipment often isn't a bargain at all. You can end up spending more money for repair and replacement of bargain equipment than you saved on the bargain in the first place. Furthermore, consider the additional cost of replacing the goldfish that died as a result of premature equipment failures.

Check the Equipment Operation

Even with reliable equipment, there may still be occasional failures. Therefore a second step in a good maintenance program is to check the equipment often to make sure it is working properly.

Heater and Thermometer
Make sure the indicator light on the heater is working and the thermostat switch is not sticking. Check the inside of the heater tube for moisture condensation. Keep the outside of the heater tube free of algae and calcium deposits (the white powdery material that precipitates on surfaces where water is heated). Anything on the outside of the tube will act as a heat insulator and prevent the heater from working properly.

For safety, always unplug the heater before removing it from the aquarium. If it has been on, unplug it and let it cool for a few minutes before taking it out of the water. Never plug in the heater when it is out of the water. These precautions will help avoid cracked heater tubes and electrical shocks.

Another good habit to develop is that of looking at the thermometer every time you look at the aquarium to make sure the temperature is where it should be. If it is off a bit, you may be able to head off trouble before it starts.

Air System
The air system should be checked every every so often. Airstones tend to become clogged with algae and salt deposits, and air hoses can become kinked. Both of these problems put backpressure on the airpump. Eventually this will cause the pump diaphragm to leak and can ruin other pump parts as well. The pump diaphragm can be checked for air leaks without taking the pump apart. Simply replace the airstone with a fresh one and unkink the air hose. If this does not restore the lost air pressure, the diaphragm is probably leaking. A replacement diaphragm can be purchased where you bought the airpump. It is inexpensive and easy to replace. For a nominal charge some fish shops will replace it for you. As a preventive measure, it is a good idea to replace the diaphragm once a year, even if it doesn't seem to be leaking.

Filter System
Check your filter at least once a week. Growths of algae and slimy dirt deposits clog air and water tubes, reducing the flow of air and water. If the filter floss

becomes too packed with dirt, a loss of water circulation results. Filter bed materials should be changed periodically. When replacing the floss, be sure to leave a small piece of the dirty floss in the filter. This helps quickly re-establish the all-important biological filtering action in the new floss. Without saving some of the old filter floss, the aquarium tends to become a bit cloudy for a few days after the filter is cleaned. The cloudiness comes from another species of bacteria that temporarily takes over until the bacteria that inhabit the floss fibers become re-established.

If you have an undergravel filtering system, the top of the gravel bed should be gently stirred every so often. This prevents the gravel from packing down too tightly and restores full circulation of water and oxygen through the gravel bed. Even without an undergravel filtering system, a minimum amount of biological filtering action occurs in the gravel bed if water is allowed to circulate through the gravel, and occasionally stirring it restores that circulation. Don't stir the gravel any deeper than about ¼ inch (6 or 7 millimeters) however, for deeper stirring may disturb the biological action in the gravel, and could also cause the water to become temporarily cloudy.

How often to stir the gravel or replace the filter floss or carbon is a question that is not easily answered with a fixed formula. The answer depends on the size of the aquarium, how many goldfish live in it, how big they are, how often they are fed, what they are fed, water temperature, the amount of light the tank re-ceives, the kind of filter, the efficiency of the filtering system, the amount of aeration, the amount of water circulation, and the amount of water that is periodically changed. A general rule is that the filter material should be replaced about every two weeks, but if it is not clogged, there is no reason to replace it. The top layer of gravel should be stirred at about the same frequency. This will help prevent the gravel from becoming foul and killing the plant roots.

After your goldfish aquarium is set up for a few months and a regular feeding routine is established, you will be able to develop your own maintenance schedule, one that suits the particular conditions of your aquarium.

Emergency Supplies

It pays to have certain emergency supplies in case the fish store is closed when a problem occurs. An experienced aquarist always has on hand extra filter floss and carbon, an extra airstone, extra pump diaphragms or a pump repair kit, an extra heater or replacement heat element, a bottle of water dechlorinator, and a few basic medications and disinfectants, which are discussed in the chapter on diseases. Also keep an inexpensive pH test kit handy for checking suspicious water chemistry.

Water Changes

It is not possible to place too much emphasis on the importance of regular partial water changes. Unlike a natural lake or river, an aquarium is a closed system—that is, it does not have fresh-water continuously flowing into it. The only freshwater the aquarium gets is what you add. Similarly, there is no water flow out of the aquarium carrying away fish wastes, uneaten food, dead plant leaves, and dead fish, except what you take out. As accumulating waste materials decompose or rot, they give off poisonous and noxious chemicals such as ammonia and carbon dioxide.

While a good filtering system removes a lot of these chemicals and their sources, no system is good enough to remove them all. Eventually the chemical composition of the water in a closed system will change, and the change will be unfavorable to the goldfish. These changes can be reduced or almost avoided completely by making partial water changes on some sort of a regular schedule.

Merely replacing water that has evaporated is not sufficient to overcome the chemical changes. When water evaporates at normal household temperatures the chemical wastes in it do not evaporate. So replacing the ½ gallon (2 liters) or so that has been lost due to evaporation does not really dilute the wastes very much at all.

Most experienced fishkeepers and even the fishkeepers that work in public aquariums find it is necessary to replace about ¼ to ⅓ of the aquarium water once a week in order to maintain over the long haul a stable chemical environment for the fish. It may not be necessary for you to make the change that often. The frequency of water changes, like the frequency of filter floss changes, depends on how much waste is being produced in your aquarium. The difference, however, is that you can see the waste in the filter, but you can't see what is dissolved in the water. It won't hurt your goldfish to have ¼ to ⅓ of their water replaced with fresh water once a week. In fact, it can only benefit them in the long run.

Some fishkeepers tend to procrastinate making those water changes. Then after a month or six weeks they replace ¾ of the water at one time. This usually leads to trouble, and often brings the goldfish to the surface gasping for air. Let's see why this happens. As the concentration of chemical wastes in the water increases, the water tends to become more acidic than normal. When water is acidic, ammonia that is accumulating in the tank is locked up in another form that is harmless to fish. When the water suddenly changes from an acidic to a neutral or alkaline composition, as it would if ¾ of it were suddenly replaced, a lot of the locked up ammonia is released as free ammonia. Free ammonia is poisonous to fish, and this is what causes them to gasp at the surface. For this reason water changes must be made in small amounts at a time. Changing ¼ to ⅓ of the aquarium water regularly every week usually prevents any kind of chemical change that is harmful to goldfish. You might be able to stretch this to every two weeks if you have only a few goldfish in a large aquarium.

When water changes are made, be sure

the water being added is about the same temperature as that which is already in the aquarium. Otherwise the sudden temperature change that might occur could cause temperature shock in the goldfish, especially if it is a change downward.

If only ¼ to ⅓ of the water is being changed, it is not necessary to add chlorine remover to the water. The water that is already in the tank will sufficiently dilute the chlorine in the new water to make it harmless to the goldfish.

A plastic bucket and a siphon hose are all that is needed for water replacement. Bend the hose into a U shape and fill it with water either under the tap or by submersing it in the aquarium. The bucket is placed on the floor below the aquarium. With your thumbs closed tightly over both ends of the water-filled hose, place one end of the hose in the aquarium and aim the other end at the bucket, keeping it below the aquarium. Take your thumbs off both ends of the hose at the same time and gravity will start the siphon. The best hose to use is one having an inside diameter of about ¼ inch (6 or 7 millimeters). A piece of garden hose has a much larger inside diameter and allows the water to flow out too fast to be controlled. The correct diameter siphon hose is another product that can be purchased where you buy your aquarium and your goldfish. The same bucket can be used to refill the aquarium, using the technique described in the section of this book on setting up the aquarium, to avoid uprooting plants.

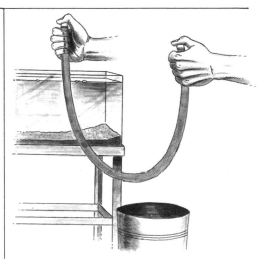

Using a siphon hose and plastic bucket for water changes. Bend the hose into a U shape and fill it with water. Then with thumbs closed tightly over both ends, place one end of the hose in the aquarium and aim the other end at the bucket. Take your thumbs off both ends at the same time and gravity will start the siphon.

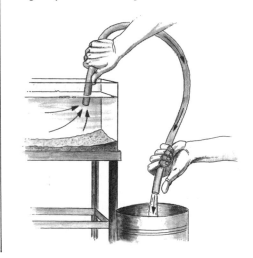

Aquarium Maintenance and Disease Prevention

Foods and Feeding

The correct feeding of goldfish is another important aspect of good aquarium management. Most goldfish varieties, some more so than others, have a tendency to overeat. It is not uncommon to see a goldfish gorge itself with so much food that afterward it can't even swim normally. In fact, it may just sink to the bottom and rest there until some of the food passes through its body.

When goldfish overeat they produce more wastes than normal. If they overeat all the time, they will soon be producing more wastes than your filtering system can handle. Even weekly partial water changes cannot compensate for this much waste, and the aquarium will soon be polluted beyond the goldfishes' tolerance. When feeding your goldfish, always keep this axiom in mind: *A slightly hungry goldfish is usually a very healthy goldfish.*

How Much Food?

Goldfish should *never be given more food than they can eat in five minutes.* This includes the time they spend picking food from the bottom of the tank. It is perfectly all right to feed them two or three times a day, although it usually isn't necessary, but never give them in one feeding more than they can eat in five minutes.

Young growing goldfish should be fed two or three times a day, but older goldfish should not be given that much food. Like any other animal, an overfed goldfish can become fat and lethargic. In such a condition, it cannot easily escape attacks from rivals, and therefore it is more likely to be injured. In general, an overfed goldfish is not as well able to resist trauma and disease as is a slimmer, more active goldfish. An older or mature goldfish should not be fed more than once a day. In fact, it will not starve if it is fed only once every other day or even every third day. On such a feeding schedule an older goldfish is likely to remain healthy and active for many years beyond its sexual maturity.

If you are feeding new goldfish for the first time, it is difficult to know how much food they will clean up in five minutes. The best way to begin is to give them just a little bit of food and watch how long it takes them to finish it. If only a minute or so has elapsed, give them a little bit more, and watch them clean it up. Continue to repeat the feeding this way until they have been eating for five minutes. Continue feeding the fish this way for a few days, until you have firmly determined how much food they will eat in five minutes. Then you can confidently give them the whole amount at one time and be pretty well assured that there will be none left over for you to clean out.

If, for one reason or another, all the food does not get eaten, the leftover food must not be allowed to remain in the aquarium, as it will begin to decompose and give off noxious chemicals almost immediately. Leftover food should be siphoned out of the aquarium as soon as possible, using the same siphon hose and bucket that is used to make partial water

Aquarium Maintenance and Disease Prevention

changes. In siphoning out leftover food, you will naturally lose a little bit of water from the aquarium. This should be made up with fresh tap water. If you follow the feeding regimen suggested here, cleaning up uneaten food should not have to be part of your regular maintenance routine. For the sake of safety, however, you should make it a habit to always check the aquarium for uneaten food after your goldfish have been fed.

Food Variety
Even goldfish can become "bored" with the same food day after day. There are, however, other more important reasons for feeding your goldfish a variety of different foods. Most commercially prepared fishfoods are floating flakes made up of a variety of meat and vegetable substances. These foods provide a wide variety of vitamins and minerals that fulfill most of your goldfishes' nutritional requirements. No one food preparation, however, despite any manufacturer's claim, can provide all of your goldfishes' nutritional needs all of the time.

Young growing goldfish do not have the same nutritional requirements as mature goldfish. They require more protein and more of certain minerals, such as calcium and phosphorous that are crucial for proper bone growth, than do older fish. Goldfish that are about to spawn (lay eggs) need more of the special dietary components that promote the development of eggs and sperm than they do during the rest of the year or when they are too old to spawn. By offering your goldfish a variety of foods, it is very unlikely that any one particular nutritional need will be left out altogether. The variety of foods also eliminates the possibility of your goldfish suffering from any of the various diseases brought on by nutritional deficiencies.

A basic staple diet of one of the commercially prepared flake or pelleted foods should be selected as the mainstay of the diet. This food should be used most of the time, but several times a week alternate foods should be offered. Alternates should be foods that are all meat, such as brine shrimp flakes or tubifex (a relative of the earthworm) flakes, or all vegetable matter, such as vegetable flakes. Instead of prepared foods, the real thing can be offered occasionally. Most fish stores sell live tubifex worms and live brine shrimp, both of which are greedily eaten by any normal healthy goldfish. These "treats" can be purchased in one-serving quantities so that storage is no problem. Another treat, and probably one of the most all around nutritional foods you can give your goldfish, is live earthworms. Small earthworms can be collected on rainy days from areas where herbicides (weed killers) have not been used recently. They should be washed in cold running water before being fed to your goldfish. If your goldfish are large enough to take them without choking, the worms can be fed whole. If not, the worms can be cut into small pieces, using a single-edge razor blade or a sharp knife. While chopped earthworms may not sound very appetizing to you, they will be greatly appreciated by your goldfish. This

61

is evidenced by the feeding frenzy they go into when offered such foods.

Almost any food you eat that is not greasy and not spiced can be offered to your goldfish. For example, they can be given occasional feedings of finely crumbled mild cheddar cheese, chopped hamburger meat, chopped shrimp, clam, or lobster, and small pieces of boiled spinach or other soft vegetables. All of these items should be used only as occasional treats, because it is more difficult to clean up leftover foods of these types than it is to clean up leftover prepared fishfoods.

The combination of all the food items mentioned here, if used with good judgment, will provide your goldfish with a well-balanced diet that will prevent them from becoming obese. This diet will keep your goldfish active and disease-resistant. It will also promote good growth in young goldfish and promote spawning in young breeders.

Do You Need Scavengers?

Contrary to popular belief, scavengers, such as snails and catfish do not eat the droppings of fish. In fact, they contribute their own droppings to the waste accumulations in the aquarium. Scavengers are generally bottom feeders and are good at finding bits of food that are left behind by the fish in the aquarium. Most goldfish varieties, however, are also well adapted to feeding from the bottom of an aquarium, and they are just as good as most scavengers at finding bits of food that have become concealed behind rocks and plants. Scavengers in a goldfish aquarium therefore do little for the goldfish except provide them with unneeded competition for food, oxygen, and space.

Catfish are generally better aquarium scavengers than snails, but most of those available for aquarium use are tropical species that require warmer water than that required by goldfish. Some *Corydoras* species—for example, the green *C. aeneus*—can tolerate a water temperature of 68° to 70°F (20–21°C). Unfortunately, the fish is not very active at that temperature, and so the purpose of having it in the tank as a scavenger is defeated. Furthermore, if the temperature drops to 65 or 60°F (18 or 11°C), goldfish are relatively unaffected, but the catfish will not live very long at that temperature.

While many species of snails can tolerate the cooler temperature of a goldfish aquarium, they cause other problems that make good aquarium management difficult. Most snails are voracious plant eaters and will destroy most aquarium plants almost as fast as you can buy them and put them in the aquarium. Some species of snails, such as the common red ramshorn or the common pond snail, reproduce so quickly and efficiently that it doesn't take very long for them to completely overrun the aquarium. Furthermore, snails are not active animals. They move slowly and spend a great deal of time completely withdrawn into their shells. When they are withdrawn, it is difficult to tell whether they are resting or dead. If they haven't moved for a couple of days, they are probably dead. The only way to tell is to remove them from the aquarium and smell them. If they give off a noxious odor, they are indeed dead. Meanwhile, between the time they died and the time you detected their death their decomposing bodies have contributed toward contamination of the aquarium water.

If all of the other suggestions made in this book for good aquarium management are followed, there is no need at all for scavengers, either snails or catfish, in a goldfish aquarium.

Avoid Crowding

Anything you can do to eliminate potentially stressful situations for goldfish will help prevent them from contracting diseases. One of the most stressful situations for goldfish is a crowded aquarium. Crowding causes wastes to be produced at a rate that is beyond the cleaning capacity of your filtering system. Crowding also produces behavioral problems in goldfish. Most become more aggressive, especially at feeding time. There will always be some that are more timid, and in a crowded situation the timid goldfish will not get their share of the food. This results in faster growth for the aggressive feeders and more intense aggression toward the smaller goldfish. In short, the overall result of crowding is that goldfish are chemically and behaviorally stressed and are much more sensitive to the attacks of disease-causing organisms and parasites.

Moving and Handling

Moving goldfish can trigger an outbreak of disease in an aquarium. The few days immediately following a move is the time goldfish are most likely to become diseased. In other words, simply bringing goldfish home from the pet shop can be hazardous to their health if they are not handled properly. It is not uncommon for a fishkeeper to buy some healthy goldfish, bring them home and put them into an aquarium that already has some healthy goldfish in it, and find a few days later that every goldfish in the aquarium has white-spot disease. This happens because moving goldfish from one aquarium to another is a traumatic experience that weakens fish, making them

Gradually changing the chemistry of the water in the bag to that of the aquarium water helps to minimize the trauma of moving for the goldfish.

Aquarium Maintenance and Disease Prevention

more susceptible to disease. If being netted out of the water isn't traumatic enough for a goldfish, consider the trauma of being dropped into a crowded plastic bag with very little oxygen in it and no filtering system in it, or the trauma of being carried outside where the temperature of water may drop considerably in a few minutes, or of being jogged and sloshed around in the bag while traveling home in a car or bus, and finally of being dropped into another aquarium in which the water might be of an entirely different chemical composition or a drastically different temperature. Is it any wonder that healthy goldfish can so easily become diseased after they are brought home?

There are, however, a number of things you can do to minimize the trauma of moving a goldfish from one aquarium to another. When you are bringing the goldfish home from the store, have the dealer wrap the plastic bags in which the goldfish are packed in a double or triple layer of newspaper or in double or triple paper bags. Do not take the plastic bags out of the wrappers or paper bags in the sunlight. Goldfish do not have eyelids that can be closed when they are moved from the dark into bright light. Once they are home, remove the plastic bags from the wrappers, and float the bags in your aquarium. (You may want to remove a bit of the aquarium water first to make room for the bags.) This will gradually equalize the temperature of the water in the bag to that in the tank. This usually takes about 15 minutes. After the temperatures are equalized, open the bag

and pour about a cupful of water from the aquarium into the bag. This allows the chemistry of the water in the bag to gradually change to that in the aquarium. Close up the bag and let it float for another 10 or 15 minutes. Then open the bag and scoop about a cupful of water out of the bag and discard it. *Do not* dump it in your aquarium. Take another cupful of water from the aquarium and pour it into the bag to further equalize the water chemistry. Close up the bag and let it sit for another 10 or 15 minutes. Now it is time to put the goldfish in the aquarium. The best way to do this is to gently pour the contents of the plastic bag, including the fish, into a fish net held over the sink, not over the aquarium. Then put the net containing the goldfish into the aquarium, and let the goldfish swim out of it. The idea of discarding the water from the bag rather than pouring it into your aquarium is to protect your aquarium from any free-floating disease organisms that might be in the water from the fish store.

If you are moving goldfish from one aquarium to another at home, the same procedure for equalizing the water temperature and chemistry should be followed. The same is true if you are making a water change in a fishbowl. No sudden change of temperature or water chemistry should be allowed to take place. By following these procedures for bringing new goldfish home or moving them from one container into another, you will minimize the trauma and shock and reduce the chances of your goldfish becoming ill as a result of the move.

Aquarium Maintenance and Disease Prevention

Know Your Goldfish

As a beginning fishkeeper you may not recognize a mistake when you've made one, and the only way you'll know it is when something goes wrong with your goldfish. The only way to know when something is wrong is to know how your goldfish behave when there are no problems. For example, you should know how widely spread your goldfish normally hold their fins. Some spread them wider than others merely because of the size of the fins. When a goldfish clamps its fins close to its body, that is usually a sign of trouble. It indicates the fish is under stress for one reason or another. Some goldfish normally swim in an oblique or head-down position, while others normally swim in a perfectly horizontal position. If one that normally swims horizontally suddenly begins to swim head-down, suspect there is trouble, because the goldfish is having trouble controlling its buoyancy. Watch your fish for a while to determine how fast they normally breathe. You can tell this by observing how fast their gill covers move in and out. By knowing what their normal breathing rate is, you'll know if they are breathing too fast or too slow. Either way, abnormal breathing is a sign of trouble. Notice their activity at various times during the day. If they are usually active during most of the day, be suspicious that something is wrong if they spend long periods of time during the day simply hovering in one spot or resting on the bottom. Be familiar with your goldfishes' normal coloration. A faded or washed out appearance during the day is an early sign of trouble. Watch your fish eat. Notice how vigorously they go after the food. If their level of activity at feeding time slows down, or if you find leftover food that you didn't find before, be suspicious that something has gone awry. If the goldfish mouth their food and spit it out or refuse food altogether, something is definitely wrong.

One of the best ways of preventing a disease from gaining a foothold in an aquarium is to watch your fish closely as often as possible. Watch your goldfish while you are feeding them, watch them while you're changing water, watch them when you're turning the lights on and off, and watch them when you're simply sitting in front of the aquarium enjoying them. Learn their normal behavior while you are watching for abnormal behavior. Early recognition of trouble is a vital and essential part of a good aquarium management program.

Summary

Before describing the diseases of goldfish and their cures, let's summarize the components of a good aquarium management program which, if closely followed, will prevent most of these diseases.

1. Equipment failures can be the cause of some diseases. Pass on bargain equipment, and buy better-quality equipment, which is less likely to prematurely fail.
2. Check your aquarium equipment often to

make sure it is working properly.

3. Change filter materials before water flow becomes blocked, and keep some of the dirty filter floss to prevent interruption of the biological filtering cycle.

4. Stir the top ¼ inch (6 or 7 millimeters) of the gravel bed every two weeks to restore full water circulation in the gravel.

5. Keep emergency supplies on hand, such as extra filter floss, airstones, a pump repair kit, water dechlorinator, and a pH test kit.

6. Replace ¼ to ⅓ of the aquarium water every week with fresh tap water of the same temperature.

7. Never feed goldfish more than they can clean up in five minutes.

8. Vary the diet as much as possible.

9. Avoid the use of snails or other aquarium scavengers.

10. Don't crowd goldfish. They need plenty of space for proper growth and compatible behavior.

11. Move goldfish as little as possible, and if it is necessary to move them, avoid sudden changes of water temperature or water chemistry.

12. Know your goldfish. Know and understand their normal behavior so you can recognize abnormal behavior as an early sign of trouble.

If this maintenance program is followed strictly and regularly, no more than 15 to 20 minutes of your time should be required each week to keep your goldfish growing, healthy, and long-lived.

RECOGNITION AND TREATMENT OF DISEASES

Let us now assume that in spite of all the precautions and preventive measures you've taken, something goes wrong in your aquarium. It happens even to the experts once in a while. Sometimes fish health problems simply cannot be avoided.

Illnesses from Polluted Water and Acidosis

Suppose you notice that your goldfish are breathing more rapidly than normal and are rubbing themselves against objects in the aquarium. These are early symptoms of white-spot disease and also signs that the chemistry of the aquarium water has gone askew. If you see no white spots on the goldfish, or any other sign of disease, check the water chemistry. Let's suppose that using your pH test kit you have detected a drop in the pH from the normal 7.0 (neutral) to 6.4, which is fairly acidic. The first thing to do is restore the pH to normal.

If the pH has not dropped too far, and 6.4 is not too far, this can be accomplished with several partial water changes made over a day or two. The addition of fresh high-quality carbon to your box filter or power filter will also help increase the pH by binding up some of the organic acids that have caused the pH to drop. The pH can also be raised by adding sodium bicarbonate to the water. The addition of chemicals, however, is the least desirable approach to the problem, for the correction is only temporary, and the continued use of chemicals can upset the chemical balance in the goldfishes' bodies. This can bring on a whole host of additional symptoms.

For the purpose of this example, let's assume that elevating the pH of the water cured the goldfishes' symptoms. Now you must find out why the pH dropped, so you can prevent it from happening again. The most likely reason is excessive organic decomposition. Perhaps a goldfish has died and its decomposing remains are hidden behind the plants. Perhaps there are some hidden pockets of uneaten food that have accumulated somewhere. If these are the problems, they are easily corrected. Simply remove the rotting material from the aquarium. Suppose, though, the problem is in the gravel bed itself. Perhaps the gravel bed is clogged with organic debris. Sometimes, if the problem is not too bad, the gravel can be cleaned sufficiently by stirring it up and siphoning out the dirt along with some of the aquarium water. You should try that before breaking down the aquarium and starting all over again.

The plastic bucket mentioned earlier is a good place to keep the goldfish while the aquarium gravel is being cleaned. Fill the bucket about half full with water from the aquarium (before the gravel is stirred up), and add enough fresh tap water of the same temperature to fill it about ¾ full. Connect an airstone to your airpump and use it to vigorously aerate the water in the bucket. Gently net the goldfish into the bucket. Keep the bucket tightly covered to prevent the goldfish from

Recognition and Treatment of Diseases

jumping out. They are likely to try jumping out because of the crowded conditions in the bucket and their own frightened condition. Once the aquarium is set up again, follow the procedure outlined for moving the goldfish back into it, but use the water from the bucket in the aquarium to dilute the new water you'll be adding as you wash the gravel. This will help minimize shock to the goldfish caused by the transfer.

Now you must find out why the gravel became clogged. It happened either because the aquarium was too crowded and there was too much waste being produced, or because the fish were being overfed, and too much waste and excess food accumulated in the gravel bed. It was probably a combination of both. As a solution, keep fewer goldfish in the aquarium and feed them less food less often.

If the pH drop had continued much longer, your goldfish might have become victims of acidosis, which is one of the results of prolonged exposure to overly acidic water. When acidosis occurs, other symptoms usually become evident. Bloody streaks sometimes show on the fin bases and around the nostrils, eyes, mouth, and anus. This is also a symptom of certain bacterial infections but not when accompanied with extremely rapid breathing and wild dashing about the aquarium. In goldfish suffering from acidosis the very slightest provocation drives them into seemingly mad behavior. If the goldfish has not bashed itself to death on a rock or against the side of the aquarium, it falls to the bottom or into the crotch of a plant, completely exhausted. Breathing then slows down and is extremely labored.

If the condition has gone this far, water changing and pH adjustment is not enough. To begin with, aeration should be increased, but it should not be so strong that it produces a water current which further exhausts the goldfish. Feeding should be terminated. The lights should be turned out, and all sides of the aquarium should be covered with black or dark paper, so that all light is shut out of the aquarium. This should all be done after the aquarium is quickly cleaned out and the water changed. After three or four days the paper can be gradually removed, and then moderate feeding can begin. With good care the goldfish can be completely restored to good health in about a week.

White-Spot Disease

If you have determined that there are no chemical problems in the aquarium, rapid breathing and scratching on objects in the aquarium can indicate that the goldfish have contracted white-spot disease, or ich. (Ich is a shortened form of the scientific name of the organism that causes the disease.) Examine the goldfish closely for encysted parasites that look like white grains of salt or sugar. If the disease has not yet progressed far, the cysts may be difficult to find. Since light usually passes through the fins and the cysts are opaque (solidly colored), they will be obvious on the fins, especially if the light comes from behind the goldfish. If the disease progresses, the fins, body, and gills will be covered with encysted parasites.

Ich is one of the most common and persistent diseases of aquarium fish. It seems to be brought on most often by a sudden chill but can begin following almost any kind of stressful situation. In order to get rid of ich, it helps to understand the parasite's life cycle. Each cyst, or white spot, you see on a goldfish is a single living, feeding parasite that got there as a free-swimming microorganism and then attached itself to the goldfish's skin. When they first attach to the fish the parasites cannot be seen by the naked eye. After they have fed on the fish's body fluids for a day or two and have encysted themselves, they are visible as small white spots. After a few days of feeding and growing, the parasites break free from the host's body and fall to the bottom of the aquarium. In other words, some of the white spots drop off the fish. Within each unattached cyst the single-celled parasite begins to reproduce rapidly. This results within 24 hours in a cyst containing about 500 new parasites. After a day or two the cyst breaks open, releasing its load of free-swimming parasites into the water. Each new parasite then seeks out a host. This is known as the infective stage of the disease, and it is the only part of the life cycle of this parasite in which it succumbs to chemicals that are not so harsh that they kill the

host fish as well. In other words, the parasite can be killed only when it is in the free-swimming stage. When it is attached to the host or is on the bottom of the tank in the reproductive stage, any chemicals strong enough to kill the parasite will also kill the goldfish.

The total life cycle of the ich parasite lasts about five days, but treating an infected aquarium for only five days is a serious mistake. There are many parasites in the tank, and there are bound to be some in each stage of the life cycle. In order to break the cycle, each and every parasite must be exposed to the treatment during its free-swimming stage. If a parasite has just attached to the host, it may be five to seven days before its offspring are in the free-swimming stage. The treatment should therefore be continued for 10 days to be sure that all parasites have passed through the vulnerable free-swimming stage.

Malachite green is an effective ich-killing chemical that does not harm goldfish or aquatic plants if it is used correctly. It is available in fish shops under a number of different trade names. The medication should be added to the aquarium once every 24 hours in the amount recommended by the manufacturer. The treatment should be continued for no less than 10 days, and during that time ¼ to ⅓ of the water should be replaced at least every two days. The medication gives the water a slight green tint when it is first put into the tank, but after a few minutes the discoloration begins to clear.

Above: different color patterns in Ryukins, Japanese versions of the ▷
fantail.
Center: shubunkin (left), a good variety for a beginner, and pearl
scale (right)
Below: two redcaps showing different dispersal of cherry red coloring.

Antibiotics, such as tetracycline or chloramphenicol, have been effectively used by some fishkeepers for treating ich, but generally such harsh drugs are not necessary. To begin with they are quite expensive. Furthermore, they generally kill the beneficial bacteria in the filters, thus causing a new set of problems. Antibiotics should not be used for treating diseases that can be effectively treated in other simpler ways. The indiscriminant use of such drugs causes the same problem in fish that it causes in humans; that is, disease organisms easily develop mutant strains that can tolerate the drugs, thus making the drugs ineffective.

Velvet Disease

Velvet is another disease known to attack goldfish. It is very similar to ich in its life cycle. It shows up as a golden velvety coating first seen on the back of the goldfish. Like ich, it eventually spreads all over the goldfish's body and gills. Each fine grain of the velvety coating is an encysted parasite. The parasite is not as easy to detect as ich, because it is much smaller and is yellow instead of white. Furthermore, the symptoms are slower to develop.

The medication of choice for treating velvet disease is acriflavine. It is a greenish-yellow dye that is sold in fish shops under a variety of trade names. For treatment of velvet, follow the directions of the manufacturer as far as dosage is concerned, but make sure the treatment

continues full strength for no less than 10 days. The color of this medication is more permanent than malachite green, so after the treatment is completed a number of partial water changes will have to be made to dilute the greenish-yellow color.

Anchor Worm

An external parasite commonly seen on pond-raised goldfish is the anchor worm. This creature is not actually a worm at all. It is the feeding stage of a copepod called *Lernacea*. It imbeds itself in muscle and gill tissue. It is seen on goldfish as a reddish wormlike thread, about ¼ inch (6 or 7 millimeters) long, often attached to the back and sides of the fish, particularly near the fin bases. It feeds on the goldfish's body fluids and eventually destroys the muscle and gill tissue. When the parasites are imbedded in a goldfish's gills, the fish may be seen violently shaking its head in an attempt to rid itself of the parasites.

One of the few medications effective against this and other kinds of external wormlike parasites is a chemical called trichlorfon, which is marketed under several trade names like Dylox® and others, and is listed as one of the ingredients in fish medicine preparations for worm treatments.

Fin Rot

Fin rot, or tail rot, commonly plagues goldfish. Fin rot is a symptom of a

70

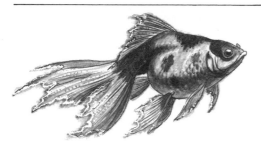

This fish has fin rot. The frayed whitish edges indicate fungal attack, a secondary infection usually following bacterial infection.

number of different diseases and can be the result of an injury. It can be a primary or secondary infection. If it is primary it is a definite symptom of a specific bacterial invasion such as that by the mycobacterium that causes columnaris disease. More often than not, however, fin rot is the result of a secondary bacterial infection such as that which occurs when a goldfish is already weakened from another disease or following an injury.

When a whitish margin begins to appear at the edge of a torn or injured fin, a bacterial infection has probably taken hold. As the disease progresses, the fins rot away, eventually reaching the fin base and then into the body tissue itself. As diseased fin tissue dies, fungus often begins to grow on the dead areas. When that happens the white margin becomes unmistakable and may appear as a fuzzy, white, cottonlike edging.

Fortunately for goldfish, destroyed fin tissue can grow back if the damage is not as deep as the fin base. Once it reaches the fin base, however, the tissue will not regenerate. The problem must be stopped before it reaches the bases of the fins.

Strong, healthy goldfish in a clean, healthy environment can sustain injuries and never show signs of fin rot. It is never wrong, however, to assume that an injured fish will become a victim of fin rot. Therefore it is not wrong to treat an injured fish for fin rot before the rot actually occurs. Such preventive treatment can head off the bacterial invasion that is likely to occur at the site of the injury.

When a goldfish is injured it should be netted out of the water and the injured area swabbed with Mercurochrome®. This is done by holding the fish firmly but gently in a wet net and swabbing the wounded area with a cotton-tipped swab dipped in the disinfectant. Be certain that the disinfectant does not run into the goldfish's eyes or gill chambers. Although that may not harm the fish, it will cause it some discomfort. Allow the disinfectant to remain on the fish for about a minute before putting it back into the water.

If the aquarium is extremely clean and contains no fish that will harass the injured fish, the fish can be placed back into the aquarium from which it came. Just to be on the safe side, though, it is better to place the injured goldfish in a separate container or fishbowl for a couple of hours before moving it to the original aquarium. A few drops of methylene blue, an aquarium disinfectant, added to the water in the holding bowl will help the goldfish recover more quickly from the trauma of the injury and the obvious trauma of the treatment. The holding bowl should be well aerated or even filtered—but not with carbon. Carbon will remove most medications from the water. Use only filter floss in the filter.

If an injured area has already been invaded by bacteria or fungus, swabbing the area with a disinfectant may not be a sufficient treatment. It may be necessary to hold the injured goldfish in a separate bowl or aquarium for a few days and administer other treatments.

A salt solution of two to four tablespoons of salt per gallon (½ to 1 tablespoon per liter) of water may be sufficient to prevent the further spread of bacterial or fungal fin rot. With this treatment, watch the goldfish for signs of distress, as different strains have different tolerances for salt. If the goldfish shows signs of stress, such as labored breathing or erratic movements, add enough fresh water to the treatment tank to relieve the stress.

If after a few days of salt treatment there are no signs of recovery, antibiotics such as tetracycline, chloramphenicol, or furanace should be used. These medications are available in most fish stores, in special preparations for aquarium use. Antibiotics should never be used in the primary or community aquarium, as they indiscriminantly kill bacteria, even the beneficial bacteria that help keep the aquarium in chemical and biological balance. Use antibiotics only in a separate treatment aquarium.

Other Diseases

The diseases discussed here are the most common ones to affect goldfish. There are many other diseases that are not as common or as easily detected. Nor are they as easily treated, for the majority of them are internal diseases that must be treated by getting medication into the fish. The only way most people can treat a fish internally is by medicating their food. The problem with that is that by the time most of these diseases are diagnosed the fish has already lost its appetite. At that point it requires special techniques beyond the capability of most fishkeepers to medicate the ailing fish.

UNDERSTANDING GOLDFISH

In order to recognize normal and abnormal behavior in goldfish, it helps to know something about their external and internal physical features. If you know, for example, how a particular kind of goldfish normally swims, and you see it swimming abnormally, understanding what specific features enable it to swim normally may give you some clues about what is wrong. Knowledge of normal physical features will also help you select the best specimens.

Shape and Structure

Goldfish varieties differ from one another mainly in the shape of the head, eyes, body, and fins. Some varieties are quite bizarre and are not typical of fish in general. The common goldfish, however, possesses all of the typical fish characteristics. We will, therefore, use it as our model to understand the shape and structure of goldfish.

Body Shape

The common goldfish has a streamlined body that is compressed from side to side. Looking at the fish from above, you can see that its head and the rear part of its body are more compressed than the middle. Looking at the fish from the side, you can see that its body is widest at about the middle. It tapers forward to a somewhat pointed, yet rounded, snout and tapers backward to a narrow tail section called the *caudal peduncle*. This tapered and compressed effect is what is meant by a streamlined shape. This shape helps the goldfish overcome friction or resistance when swimming through the water.

Skin

The body is covered with a thin outer skin called the *epidermis*. Within the epidermis are many mucus-secreting cells that produce the slime or mucus coating that covers the fish. The mucus coating helps protect the goldfish from disease-causing organisms and it also lubricates the fish, which helps it overcome the resistance of the water when it swims.

Lying under the epidermis, and largely responsible for the goldfish's color, is a layer of skin that contains pigment cells and scales. Pigment cells contain the material that gives the goldfish its color. The scales are hard and roundish, and overlap one another like the tiles or shingles on a roof. This arrangement gives the goldfish plenty of flexibility for swimming, but the hardness of the scales gives it a lot of protection against injuries.

Under the pigment and scale layer is the inner skin, which is called the *dermis*. The dermis helps keep the fish together and gives it its shape.

Fins

The fins of a goldfish play an important role in its ability to move about. Some fins aid forward and backward motion and make possible fine maneuvers such as swimming through plant thickets. Other

Understanding Goldfish

fins aid sudden bursts of speed. Some give the goldfish swimming and hovering stability, and some aid in stopping or braking forward or backward motion.

Like most fish, goldfish have two kinds of fins: median fins and paired fins. Median fins occur singly and lie in the center vertical plane of the body. In certain goldfish varieties some median fins, such as the tail or caudal fin, are split

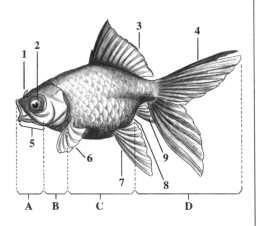

Anatomy of a goldfish

A. Mouth region ⎫
B. Gill region   ⎬ Head area
                     ⎭
C. Body
D. Tail region
1. Nostril
2. Eye
3. Dorsal fin
4. Tail, or caudal, fin
5. Lower jaw
6. Pectoral fin
7. Ventral fin
8. Anus
9. Anal fin

or doubled. These are not the same as paired fins, for they have a common base or point from which they grow out of the body. Paired fins actually occur in pairs and grow out of the body from opposite sides.

The dorsal fin is a median fin that grows out of the goldfish's back. In a healthy goldfish it is usually held erect, and it helps stabilize the fish. In other words, like the deep keel of a sailboat, it helps prevent side-to-side rolling. Some goldfish varieties have long dorsal fins that cannot be held fully erect; these drape over the side of the fish and interfere with swimming and rolling stability. Some varieties—the celestial, for example—have no dorsal fin at all and are not good swimmers.

The caudal fin is a median fin that grows out of the caudal peduncle. The caudal fin is usually forked, and it helps propel the fish forward. The deepness of the fork in the caudal fin varies from variety to variety, as does the length of the fin lobes. In some long-finned varieties there is no fork at all, and the fin hangs downward like a drape. Like the draped dorsal fin, this impairs swimming, but in the aquarium, where all the fish's needs are provided for, this makes little difference in its survival. In some varieties, the caudal fin is split or doubled; each half is usually joined along the upper edge and at the base, although in some the halves are not joined at the upper edge.

The anal fin is a median fin that grows out of the bottom of the fish but behind the anal and sexual openings. It is also a stabilizing fin, and it aids somewhat in maneuvering and swimming. In long-finned varieties this fin is usually elongated and sometimes split or doubled. When doubled the halves are joined at the base and in some strains are also joined along the rear margin of the fin.

The pelvic or ventral fins are paired fins that grow out of the lower abdomen of the goldfish ahead of the anal and sexual openings. Each fin grows from the opposite side of the central line of the abdomen and protrudes from the body at an angle. These fins act as stabilizers and as brakes to help stop forward or backward motion. They also aid in fine maneuvers. The pelvic fins are elongated in some goldfish varieties, but the elongation is rarely as exaggerated as it is in the dorsal and caudal fins.

Finally, goldfish have a pair of pectoral fins that grow out from both sides of the body, slightly behind and toward the bottom of the gill cover openings. The pectoral fins are almost always in motion, helping to stabilize the fish and aiding in tight maneuvers such as turning. The pectoral fins can be used to aid forward motion, but that occurs more in the types of goldfish that have round stubby bodies and can't swim very well. The pectoral fins are somewhat elongated in long-finned goldfish strains.

Swim Bladder

The swim bladder is an important internal organ that gives the goldfish buoyancy. Without it, the fish would sink to the bottom of the aquarium when it stopped swimming. Having buoyancy dramatically reduces the amount of energy required for swimming.

The swim bladder is a gas-filled sac that lies inside the body cavity above most of the internal organs. The amount of gas in the sac changes as the goldfish rises or sinks in the water. This gives the goldfish a great deal of maneuverability for swimming, hovering, and exploring its surroundings.

In most fish the swim bladder is a single elongated sac, but in the goldfish the sac is divided into two parts, one lying ahead of the other. In the common goldfish both parts are about equal and are shaped like stubby cigars. Because of the uniformity of the front and rear sac parts, the common goldfish can easily maintain a horizontal position when hovering. In stubby-bodied, or egg-shaped, goldfish, such as the lionhead, both parts of the swim bladder are globe-shaped, but the forward part is very small and the rear part is very large. This causes the fish to hover at a slight head-down angle, and often it even swims at that angle.

When the effects of a disease distort the swim bladder, a goldfish looses its equilibrium and may swim at an odd angle. The effects of that loss are much more drastic in egg-shaped goldfish, because the swim bladder is already highly distorted before it becomes diseased. It is not uncommon to see such a goldfish struggle to swim down through the water and then helplessly bob back up to the surface. Unfortunately, there is very little that can be done medically for such a goldfish.

Understanding Goldfish

How a Goldfish Swims

Most of a goldfish's forward motion is the result of its waving the rear half of its body and its tail back and forth. This is done by contracting groups of muscles on one side of the body while at the same time flexing or relaxing the opposite muscles on the other side of the body. This pulls the back part of the body and the tail to one side. The muscle contraction and flexion then reverses, and this pulls the back part of the body and the tail to the opposite side. This side-to-side motion pushes water behind the fish, which results in forward thrust for the fish.

One of the reasons that egg-shaped goldfish are such poor swimmers is that the rear part of the body is reduced and distorted. This results in a lack of the power needed for the fish to propel itself forward.

How a Goldfish Breathes

A goldfish breathes by using its gills to extract oxygen from the water and expel carbon dioxide into the water. The gills are located on the sides of the head, above the throat area, and are covered by gill covers, or *opercula*. The gills consist of finely divided fleshy filaments, each of which is highly profused with many tiny blood capillaries. This brings the blood very close to the surface of each filament. By a process called osmosis the blood passing through the filaments absorbs oxygen from the water passing over the

gills and by the same process gives up carbon dioxide to the water. The alternating opening and closing of the goldfish's mouth and gill covers causes water to be pumped through the mouth, past the gills, and out through the gill cover opening. The gills also serve as a means of helping the goldfish balance some of the natural chemicals in its body with those in the surrounding water. Any disease or injury of the mouth, gills, or gill covers can cause severe breathing distress or an internal chemical imbalance in the goldfish.

How a Goldfish Senses Its Surroundings

A goldfish, like a human, has special sense organs through which it learns about its surroundings.

Vision

An obvious difference between humans and fish is that fish have no eyelids. A less obvious difference is that the fish eye has no iris (the colored part in the human eye that contracts or expands to admit more or less light). In nature these differences are not a problem, because the change from darkness to daylight comes about gradually. Fish do have, built into the retina of the eye, a means of adapting from darkness to daylight, but it works very slowly and may take several hours for complete adjustment.

Because a goldfish has no means of blocking out the sudden change when an aquarium light is turned on in a dark room, it immediately dashes for cover. In an aquarium that is not heavily planted and decorated, there is no shelter from bright lights, and a sudden exposure to bright light could throw the goldfish into visual shock. If this happens often enough, the goldfish may be sufficiently weakened to become diseased. In addition, it could be injured in its frantic attempt to seek cover. The problem can be solved by remembering to open the window shades gradually on a sunny day or turn the room lights on one at a time for about 30 minutes before turning the aquarium lights on.

Science has proved that goldfish do perceive colors and shapes, but they do not see anything at a great distance very well. They are basically nearsighted, with a limited range of frontal vision. However, they do see off to the side fairly well. All of this means that vision is not one of the fish's more important senses. As an example, there is an aquarium fish known as the blind cave fish, which has evolved with no eyes at all. The fish schools, feeds, breeds, avoids enemies, and generally finds its way around as well as any sighted fish. There are several goldfish varieties in which this is also evident. For example, the celestial goldfish has a peculiar eye mutation that allows it to see only upward, yet it doesn't bump into anything, and it eats fairly well.

Smell
While the sense of smell is not as highly developed in fish as it is in some land-dwelling animals, such as the dog, it is important for most fish, including goldfish. Fish use their sense of smell to communicate with their environment. For example, it is believed to be the sense of smell that enables a migrating salmon to find its home stream at spawning time. The sense of smell is used to detect food, it plays an important role in sexual activity, and it even plays a role in schooling behavior.

The olfactory, or smell, organs are located in the nostrils. Unlike higher animals, fish nostrils do not connect to the mouth or throat. Some fish have four nasal openings, two on each side of the snout. Water passes in one opening and out the other as the fish move about. Goldfish and most freshwater fish have only two nasal openings, one on each side of the snout. Each one is a dead-end sac. Water enters and leaves the nostril through the same opening. While this may seem inefficient, it apparently works quite well. Just as polluted air causes injury to our sense of smell, polluted water injures the goldfish's olfactory sensors. Foul water can, for example, cause a goldfish to become disoriented, making it difficult for the fish to find food.

Taste
Goldfish have many taste buds, but they are not necessarily located in the tongue. Rather, they are located all over the mouth, but mostly in the lips, both inside and outside the mouth. Since the goldfish uses its mouth to explore its surroundings, this arrangement is a tremendous

help in finding food. As in most animals, the sense of taste and smell work together in helping the goldfish find its way around.

Touch

The goldfish has a tactile sense, or sense of touch. As with most fish, however, its tactile sense organs are not very highly developed. Whether or not goldfish feel pain, as we know pain, is a difficult question to answer. Fish do react negatively to negative stimuli, but the reaction may be mostly uncontrolled reflex behavior, which is like our knee-jerk response during a physical examination.

Hearing

Fish do not have external ears. Nonetheless, there is no doubt that they hear what is going on around them. As evidence, gently rap on your aquarium, and watch your goldfishes' reaction: they jump in fright. Some fish make grunting and squeaking noises during mating, feeding, or when attacking or being attacked. These noises are heard by other fish and cause them to react appropriately.

Unlike people, fish hear in several different ways. The main hearing organ lies in the head. It is similar to our inner ear in that the canals provide a sense of balance, but the inner ear of a fish has no cochlea. Instead it has a hard stone, called an *otolith*, through which sound is detected. Sound vibrations are transmitted from the water, through the fish's body, to the otolith. In some fish, including the goldfish, a series of bones called the *weberian ossicles* transmit amplified sound from the swim bladder, through the skull, to the otolith, in much the same way that sound is transmitted in our ears from the eardrum, through three small bones (the anvil, hammer, and stapes) to the cochlea.

Lateral Line System

Goldfish also detect pressure changes produced in water by sound and other vibrations. This is done through the lateral line system. Goldfish, as well as most other fish, have a lateral line, which is a system of nerve cells, called *neuromasts*, that lie in pores in a canal that runs along the side of the fish to the head. The whole system is connected to the fish's brain through the auditory nerve. Water pollution can cause disease of the lateral line system. This usually disorients the goldfish, which affects its ability to swim, feed, or do almost anything it normally does.

How a Goldfish Eats

The mouth of the goldfish is protractile. This means its jaws move outward, away from the skull, when it feeds. This enables the fish to pick morsels of food from the bottom of the aquarium without having to orient itself in a nearly vertical position.

There are a few fine teeth in the jaws that enable the goldfish to grip and tear small pieces of food. Most of the goldfish's teeth, however, are not in its jaws; they are in its throat. These are called *pharyngeal teeth*. They consist of a number of cone-shaped and molar-shaped teeth mounted on a plate in the lower part of the throat. When food passes through the gullet the lower tooth plate moves against another hard plate located in the upper part of the throat, and this grinds up the goldfish's food. This is why a goldfish does not choke when it picks up a long worm. As the worm is pulled through the mouth, it is ground up in the throat.

Do Goldfish Sleep?

Even though they cannot close their lidless eyes, goldfish do indeed sleep. Shortly after the lights go out the goldfish's colors begin to fade, and its activity slows down. Its colors do not completely fade, as they do in some fish, but the goldfish looses most of its metallic luster. A sleeping goldfish usually, though not always, sinks to a low position in the water and is usually hidden in a sheltered area of the aquarium. The goldfish does make some minor move-ments in its sleep to help retain its balance, but it does not engage in any major swimming activity.

If it is dark and the lights are suddenly turned on a goldfish will react in a startled manner and may seek further cover. During the next few minutes its colors gradually return. When the colors have returned, the goldfish begins to swim, slowly at first, until it is fully awake.

Like any other animal, goldfish need rest and sleep. If the aquarium lights are left on 24 hours a day, the goldfish will still sleep for short periods of time, but this is not enough. Eventually it will acclimate to 24 hours of light and will get an adequate amount of sleep. For a goldfish's overall health, it is not a good idea to leave the aquarium lights on 24 hours a day.

Colors in Goldfish

Most of the goldfish's color comes from a material called guanine, which is found in the scales in a crystalline form. This material gives the goldfish its characteris-tic gold metallic luster. Those goldfish having full metallic coloration are called metallic-scaled goldfish.

Some goldfish show a mottled or variegated color pattern with spots in a variety of blues, purples, reds, oranges, yellows, white, and black. The scales in these fish lack some of the metallic luster of the metallic-scaled goldfish. These are called nacreous goldfish. The partial lack of guanine crystals in the scales of these fish allows the other colors to show through.

A third color form, called matt goldfish, have no guanine crystals at all and have no luster whatsoever in the scales. These fish are usually white or cream-colored. Some goldfish can have patches showing all three types of coloration.

Black and blue or purplish colors in goldfish come from pigment cells located in the outer skin or epidermis. The colors are caused by a concentration or a dispersement in these cells of a black material called melanin. A white goldfish not only lacks guanine in the scales but also completely lacks melanin in the skin.

When goldfish first hatch out they are almost colorless. After they are a few months old they have a dull golden color. Shortly after that they begin to develop patches of reds, oranges, blues, and black. These colors continue to change as the baby goldfish grow. After six months or so the black patches begin to disappear and some of the reddish patches begin to fade. The goldfish's color usually stabilizes by the time it is a year old. Not all goldfish develop this array of colors and not all of them take a year to stabilize. All of them do, however, go through the dull color phase as babies, and some of them may not develop full permanent coloration until they are almost two years old. It is obviously futile to choose young goldfish by their color pattern, for the colors will change several times before the fish are fully grown.

Sociability in Goldfish

As a general rule goldfish are not aggressive, although larger ones tend to get more food than smaller ones. Under normal conditions goldfish do not nip at the fins of other goldfish. However, if a goldfish is injured, its tankmates may tend to pick on it.

Goldfish have a tendency to school. This behavior can be seen most readily in a pond where the goldfish have plenty of swimming room. Schooling is a random affair. There is no dominant school leader. If one goldfish wanders away from the school, the others tend to follow it, but then a different one may randomly wander, and the school will turn and follow that one. The wanderers instinctively return to the school.

The only time goldfish exhibit aggressive behavior is at breeding time. This usually follows a period of cooling and occurs when the water begins to warm. That is why goldfish kept in a pond usually breed only in the spring. During that time the males relentlessly drive or chase the females until spawning is completed. There are very few displays of rivalry between males.

Goldfish are mildly cannibalistic. They greedily devour their own eggs and often pursue and eat their own offspring. They rarely bother other species of fish that are kept with them.

By and large, goldfish are peaceful fish that spend much of their time randomly wandering around the aquarium in search of food. After a few weeks of good care and feeding they will respond to anyone who approaches the aquarium or opens the lid by gathering in a mild frenzy at the regular feeding spot.

discontinuous from body

of scale mainly

1 Orange + Black
1 Calico

b. Veiltail — elongated body like common
goldfish. Fins Full, body long + delicate.
Dorsal fin Erect / Edge Convex. Rounded
body then fantail

— Oranda — hood on head

— Telescope

calico, white, 2 orange + black
1 redcap, 1 orange + white
hood on head
2 Black Moores

(A) Tapered Body
1. Comet
2. Shubunkin - 3
3. Bristol Shubunkin;
has round Tail 3

(B) Egg Shaped Body

1. No Dorsal Fin
a. Celestial -
b. Bubble Eye -
c. Lionhead 2
d. Ranchu Iron-Tail
Bents Down

2. Dorsal Fin
a. Fantail - Moderate Length / Slightly Forked
Tail. Dorsal
b. Ryukin - high curve

2 Blue, 1 Chocolate
2 pearl scale

BREEDING GOLDFISH

There is no reliable way to determine the sex of young goldfish or of adult breeders out of breeding season. However, if you buy six young fish to raise as breeders, chances are you will have at least one of each sex. When the fish are mature, you'll be able to sex them during the spring breeding season. At that time females become swollen with ripe eggs. This is easy to see in flat-bodied strains but may be more difficult in egg-shaped varieties. The best way to determine which are females is to look at them from above. From that angle egg-laden females look much broader than males. An easier and usually more reliable way to tell their sex is to look for fish that have white pimple-like bumps on their heads and gill covers. These fish are males. The bumps are called *breeding tubercles*, and they develop just prior to the breeding season. After spawning is complete, the tubercles gradually disappear. Occasionally males fail to develop tubercles, but they are still "ripe" for spawning. A less reliable way to sex goldfish is to look at their colors. During the breeding season the colors of both sexes intensify, but especially in the males.

Pre-Spawning Preparations

A fairly long cooling period, down to 60°F (11°C) or lower, followed by a gradual warming of the water triggers breeding behavior in goldfish. This is why pond-kept goldfish breed only once a year—in the spring. When the water begins to warm, heavy feeding of a highly nutritious high-protein diet helps "ripen" the fish. Lots of live food, such as brine shrimp and worms, conditions them quickly. Thick clumps of bushy plants, such as *Myriophyllum*, serve as a spawning site.

Courtship and Spawning

Goldfish do not form pair-bonds. They are promiscuous breeders. Any male will breed with any female. When the water warms to 65° to 68°F (18° to 20°C) and the fish are "ripe," courtship begins. At first, and for a few days, males randomly chase females all over the pond or aquarium, while the colors of both sexes intensify. Then heavy driving begins, with the male relentlessly chasing the female into the plant thickets. After a few hours of intense driving, spawning begins. This consists of the male pushing the female against the plants while both fish gyrate from side to side. During the gyrations eggs and sperm are ejected into the water. As the eggs fall through the water they stick to the plants by sticky threads. After a few minutes the fish separate and the whole sequence begins all over again, starting with a strong chase. Spawning is complete in two or three hours. A large female can lay as many as 10,000 eggs. For short lulls during spawning and immediately afterward both fish greedily eat as many eggs as they can find. They should be removed from the pond or aquarium when spawning is over.

Breeding Goldfish

Stages in the development of a goldfish

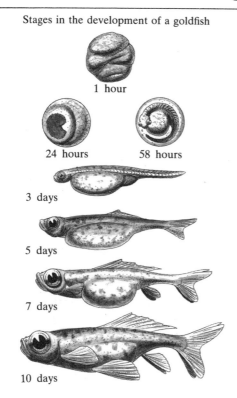

1 hour

24 hours   58 hours

3 days

5 days

7 days

10 days

Embryo Development

Goldfish eggs look like tiny transparent bubbles. The incubation time is five to seven days, depending on temperature: five days at 70°F (21°C) and seven days at 65°F (18°C). During this time some eggs may become fungused. First they turn white, and then they begin to resemble tiny fuzzy cotton balls. The addition of disinfectants, such as acriflavine or methylene blue, to the water inhibits the spread of fungus on eggs.

After four days pigmented eyes, small pigment spots on the body, and a beating heart can be seen on the developing embryos. In addition, the embryos begin to wiggle in the eggs. By the fifth day the embryos and yolk sacs are heavily pigmented. On the fifth to seventh day the larval fish burst out of their eggs, tail first. For the next 48 hours the 1/5-inch (5 millimeter)-long larvae hang all over the plants and the sides of the aquarium or pond by sticky head glands. Then they begin to swim free and search for food.

Raising the Fry

This is the most critical time in the life of young goldfish. Most of them die at this stage for lack of food. If you intend to raise the fry, you must provide them with an abundance of fine powdered foods as well as live or frozen baby brine shrimp and microworms. You can purchase live food in most pet shops.

The larval goldfish remain almost colorless for a while, and then, after a few weeks, they become a whitish color. By the time they are two months old they begin to take on a pale yellow sheen. From that time on their color changes continuously until they reach adulthood.

Because of the difficulty of raising the fry, breeding of goldfish should not be attempted by new fishkeepers. I personally think that beginners should concentrate all their efforts on learning to understand and care for goldfish. After six months to a year of successful experience, goldfish breeding can be attempted and will probably be successful.

GOLDFISH POOLS

The last subject to be dealt with in this book is the outdoor goldfish pool. Construction of a pool involves the investment of a great deal of time and money. The beginner should therefore first learn how to care for goldfish in an aquarium before making the investment in a pool. Mistakes in an aquarium are, by comparison, cheap to correct, and if the beginner ends up abandoning the hobby, not much has been lost.

Protecting the Goldfish from Temperature Extremes

Protection of the goldfish is the most important thing to keep in mind when planning a pool. During the winter the goldfish must be protected from being frozen into the ice. This is done by making the pool deep enough to prevent it from being frozen to the bottom. Also, you can transfer the fish to an indoor aquarium for the winter. Another danger with a shallow pool is that it tends to overheat during the summer. Making it deep enough may also prevent overheating. A goldfish pool should generally be no less than 2 feet (60 centimeters) deep and should have a deeper area of 3 to 4 feet (90 to 120 centimeters) in the center or at one end. Although sloping the entire bottom of the pool to form the deeper part is ideal for the goldfish, it is not necessary. A deeper section can be made merely by building a trench 2 feet (60 centimeters) deep by 2 feet (60 centimeters) wide across the center or one end of the pool. The deepest part is where the drain should be located.

Another way to protect the pool from overheating is to shade it. This can be done in a number of different ways, and a combination of all of the methods does the best job. The pool can be shaded by building it in the shadow of your house or some tall dense trees or shrubs. Other tall plants, such as canias and lilies, vine-covered trellises, and solid or vine-covered fences can be located close enough to the pool to serve as decorative landscaping as well as shade for the pool. Also, a permanent or movable leanto, one that can be adjusted to the position of the sun, can be built over the pool.

Thoroughly planting the pool itself also protects it from overheating. One of the best shade-producing plants is the water lily, of which there are many lovely varieties to choose from. The leaves of water lilies are broad flat pads. Not only do they protect the pool from overheating but they also provide shelter for the goldfish. Goldfish swim under lily pads to get away from bright sun, to hide from enemies, or simply to rest. Water lilies are generally planted in pots that are filled with rich soil and covered with a top layer of gravel to keep the soil in the pot. They can be located anywhere in the pool and will spread their pads and beautiful flowers over the surface. Furthermore, as the summer progresses and the position of the sun changes, potted water lilies can be moved about to continue to provide shade all summer long. Water hyacinths are also good plants for goldfish pools. They have large bladders that allow them to float on the surface where they multiply rapidly and spread out to provide lots of shade. An added benefit of the water hyacinth is that its bushy hanging roots provide shelter for the goldfish as well as an excellent place for them to spawn. There are many other plants suitable for the goldfish pool that provide shade, shelter, and spawning sites. A trip to the shop of a knowledgeable fish dealer to discuss your pool plans will turn up other plant varieties as well as many other good and practical ideas for managing a goldfish pond.

Protecting the Goldfish from Predators

One final major problem that must be considered in planning a goldfish pool is how to protect the goldfish from predators such as snakes, birds, raccoons, weasels, cats, frogs, turtles, predator water beetles and *Dytiscus* beetles, and insect larvae. Most predatory terrestrial animals can be kept out of the yard by good solid fences. Snakes, however, can find their way under or around almost any fence. Fortunately there aren't that many terrestrial fish-eating snakes to worry about. Predatory birds present a problem that is almost impossible to deal with. Covering the yard or the pool itself with netting is a solution but not a very good one. Some hobbyists have tried scarecrows and have had limited success. The best answer to the problem is to have plenty of plants for the goldfish to hide under, and hope they can escape fast enough.

Protecting goldfish from predatory insects, such as water beetles or *Dytiscus* beetles, and predatory insect larvae, such as dragonfly larvae or various kinds of beetle larvae, is even more difficult than protecting them from birds, because fish cannot hide from these predators. The only thing you can do is watch for evidence of the insects in your pond and treat the water with a sufficiently strong dose of copper sulfate, which kills most invertebrates rather quickly. It is best to remove the fish from the pond or pool while treating the water. After the water has been at least partially replaced to dilute the chemical, the fish can be returned to it.

Setting Up the Pool

To begin your pool project you must decide whether you want to use a prefabricated plastic pool or want to construct a poured concrete pool. If a small plastic pool is your choice, plans should be made to drain it every fall, for it will not be deep enough to survive the winter without freezing to the bottom, which can destroy the pool as well as kill the goldfish. A plastic pool should be placed over a deep bed of coarse gravel or very solid soil for support.

If a poured concrete pool is your choice, your pool can be designed to any shape and depth you wish. The walls of the pool should be at least 4 inches (10 centimeters) thick up to a depth of 2 feet (60 centimeters) and should be 1 inch (2.5 centimeters) thicker for each additional foot (30 centimeters) of depth. The bottom should be 4 to 6 inches (10 to 15 centimeters) thick, depending on the depth of the pool and the firmness of the underlying substrate. The bottom of the pool should be sloped to one end to make cleaning easier. Small level platforms can be built into the sloped bottom of a concrete pool to hold the water lily pots. There should be no rough projections in the walls or bottom that could injure the goldfish.

The concrete must be "cured" before putting fish in the pool. This is done by filling the pool with water and letting it stand for a few days. In addition to leeching excess lime out of the concrete, this also allows time for leaks to show up so they can be repaired before the pool is finally filled. After a few days, empty the pool and scrub the concrete down with a mild acid, such as vinegar, to neutralize any excess lime. The pool should be rinsed out several times and finally filled. Just to be on the safe side, this whole process can be repeated once or twice before finally filling the pool and putting fish in it.

By way of special equipment, a well-kept pool should be filtered. This requires a special pool filter and submersible water pump made for that purpose. You should also consider how the pool is to be drained for cleaning. A standpipe should be kept in the drain to allow excess water from rainstorms and runoff to flow gently out of the pool. A screen cap over the top of the standpipe will prevent fish from being sucked into the drain.

The idea of a backyard goldfish pond or pool is indeed an exciting one. This brief chapter will at least give you some ideas to think about for a few months, while through aquarium experiences you learn how to handle and understand your goldfish.

Happy fishkeeping!

Index